MW00365625

Loving for Life 48
Building a Convenant Marriage

LeeAnn Smucker Rawlins

Loyal Publishing
www.loyalpublishing.com

Cover design by Bill Chiaravalle

Loving For Life
Copyright © 1999 by LeeAnn Smucker Rawlins
Loyal Publishing, Inc.
P.O. Box 1892, Sisters, OR 97759

ISBN 1-929125-03-8
(previously ISBN 0-88419-232-6)

Printed in the United States of America.

99 00 01 02 03 04 05 06 07 / 10 9 8 7 6 5 4 3 2 1

To Willard,

my wonderful husband for twenty-four years,
whom I loved dearly.

Contents

Acknowledgments

I want to express my gratitude to David Hazard, first my editor and then my friend. Without his encouragement, I probably would not have completed this project. The Lord used him as His servant to help me.

I would like to thank so many others for their love and help in making this book possible:

Janice Rogers, for her words of encouragement to get me started on this project, and also to get it finished.

Janet Benge, for the hours she put into this book, both at the writing school we attended together and in the first editing stage, and for her love and encouragement.

My friend Carolyn Bell and my sister Vevi Schrock, for their typing help in the first stages. Also, my niece Karen Such for her help with the typing.

My son, Lonnie, who gave me my first computer lessons. What a blessing!

My two sons, Mark and Rob, who loved and encouraged me, and my many friends and family who did the same.

My dear husband, Duane, who gave me many constructive suggestions, and stood by me and showed me God's faithfulness.

And to Matt Jacobson who gave me the gift of redoing this book after ten years. Also, to Celesté Clements, Josephine Davis, and Barbara Overgaard for their help in the editing process.

Most of all, my dear Lord Jesus, who prompted me to write this book and provided just the people I needed to help me complete it.

Introduction

What Is Love?

In 1984, Glynn "Scotty" Wolfe filed for his twenty-sixth divorce and began looking for his twenty-seventh bride. A former Hollywood stunt pilot with forty children, Wolfe was proud of his place in the *Guinness Book of World Records* as the most married man on earth. He died in 1997, having been married 28 times.[1]

According to Wolfe, seventy-six-years-old at the time, his latest marriage was failing because his thirty-eight-year-old wife was never at home. "These young women," he said, "don't want to stay home, wash and iron clothes, and sweep the floor." For that reason, Wolfe decided his marriage wasn't worth saving. It wasn't doing for him what he wanted anymore.

Wolfe's casual attitude toward marriage is the epitome of today's society, which enters and exits the union on the slightest provocation. It is far too easy to get out of marriages today. The marriage vows are not taken seriously enough. We base far too much on feelings rather than on commitment. It's little wonder the sacredness of marriage has been largely lost. Forty, or possibly even fifty percent of marriages will end in divorce if current societal trends continue.[2]

Wolfe's decision to end his marriage is a reflection of his selfishness. His focus wasn't on what he could do for his wife, but on what she wasn't doing for him. Even in Christian marriages, we tend to focus on our own self-interest, asking questions like: Should I give in on this point or fight for what I want? Should I look after myself before I look after him in this situation? If I give and keep on giving, will I be taken advantage of? And behind these questions is an even deeper one: Will I choose to love despite the circumstances?

The problem with many marriages today is the couple's concept or basis of love. For many, their love is based on sexual attraction or the emotional fulfillment they get from one another. To them, it seems so right and often pushes them into marriage—a marriage based on feelings. When the sexual attraction that exists between a man and a woman is mistaken for love, the commitment to the other person is conditional. If the beauty fades, the sweet nothings cease, and the expectations fail to be met, then the marriage is over. She says, "The love is gone. I don't love him anymore. He's not meeting my needs." Unfortunately, she never knew what true love meant. Her concept of love was based on her own fulfillment and the temporal things that change.

True love puts self second. It allows for mistakes and will remain steadfast in spite of them. Love looks for ways to bless the other. Love is slow to anger. Love forgets when wrong is done. When love believes these things, we experience the romantic side of love. What is more romantic to a wife than when she has been temperamental to her husband and he responds softly to her? Or when she lashes out at him in anger and he leans over and gently kisses her on the cheek? The self-less side of love draws spouses toward one another.

Jesus demonstrated selfless love in his Sermon on the Mount when he instructed, "But whoever slaps you on your right cheek, turn the other to him also" (Matt. 5: 39 NEW KING JAMES VERSION). He went even further in his ministry here on earth by demonstrating love to those who treated him poorly: "Bless those who persecute you, bless and do not curse" (Rom. 12:14 NEW INTERNATIONAL VERSION). He laid down his life for us even though none of us deserved it. He loved us despite our indifference to righteousness. He asked us to "Love one another as I have loved you" (John 15:12 NKJV). The selflessness of Jesus' love sets a high standard by which He instructs us to love others.

Jesus' unconditional and selfless love has given us the greatest gift—eternal life. Our unconditional and selfless love for our husbands can't bestow this great gift, but our Christlikeness can bring us closer together. A person, writing anonymously said, "As we grow closer to God, we grow closer to each other." It's so true. As we align our character more with His, we will draw our husbands closer to us. That is the greatest benefit of selfless love.

Not long ago, I was at a wedding for a groom named Jim. The pastor said, "Let's take Jim's name and use it as an acronym to help you in a given situation. J - just, I - imitate, M - me." If couples would learn to imitate Jesus through every trial, their relationships would be so much better.

With the false definition of love that is pumped into homes by the media, even Christians have a problem with truly loving like 1 Corinthians 13. Jesus' example needs to be the compass by which we genuinely love our husbands.

I have written this book to encourage others to love their husbands for life. Without love, living with anyone is difficult at best. Love brings life. Perhaps you are living with a husband who doesn't meet your expectations. Maybe you don't feel a true unity with your man. Maybe you haven't yet realized how your love for your husband—or lack of it—affects your children. Yes, every aspect of your life can be influenced by the love you demonstrate in your marriage.

In all these areas, I can say that I've been blessed, not because I'm good, but because God is good. When He tells us to love, we can only follow His Word. He is ever present to help us in the difficult times.

He is the Lord of life and the Lord of love. He has encouraged me with a deep, but simple truth about our marriage relationships, a truth on which this book is founded. It is simply this: You cannot lose by loving. Let me show you how His love can spill over and bless your entire life.

In the following chapters I want to share with you the lessons I have learned from the joys and hurts of my experience with marriage. I want to show you the joy that comes from choosing to love despite the circumstances. This is not wholly my personal story, though I'll relate personal experiences. Instead, this book is a result of my desire to show you, as a wife, the benefits of loving your husband.

Chapter One

Love Never Ends

My dear sweet husband, Willard, was raised on a farm in a beautiful valley near Eugene, Oregon. His family was Mennonite. As so many of the rural Mennonite boys did, he left school after the eighth grade to work on the family farm.

What Willard lacked in formal education was more than made up for in practical wisdom and a certain inner quality—integrity. People who knew Willard would tell you he lived what he believed and was always good to his word. He soon gained the respect of farmers all over the valley.

I first met Willard at a church party. I'd come from Idaho to study at a Mennonite school. He was tall, handsome, and athletic, with dark hair and a cute crooked grin. The first thing that attracted me, to be honest, was his quietness. He was almost shy.

As soon as we began to date, however, I saw at once how loudly his life spoke for what he believed. I'd been brought up with the stability of a loving Christian home, and it was so important for me to see how much Willard respected his parents. He also loved church and attended regularly. I fell deeply in love with him. We were soon engaged and a year later, in November 1960, we were married.

After our marriage, I continued to be impressed by Willard's respect for his parents. He was twenty at the time, and we were ready to strike out on our own. But out of respect for his father, he willingly honored the family custom that each son work at home until he turned twenty-one.

As I said, Willard was a man of his word. He was not a man of lots of words, but when he spoke people listened. His friends jokingly called him "E.F. Hutton." When he believed something, he lived it. If he said he would do something, you could count on his doing it whatever the cost.

You would think that such an ideal-sounding young man and an in-love young woman would have a perfect life together. No problems, no disagreements. I think we had a beautiful marriage, and it brought into this world three wonderful young men—our sons, Mark, Lonnie, and Rob. But our marriage had its struggles. No marriage, no matter how ideal the spouses, is without its difficult times.

Learning to Love

It was Saturday morning—quite like all other Saturday mornings. It was a crisp March morning in Oregon, in 1984. The phone beside our comfortable waterbed rang waking us up. It had been a wonderful night together. The security of our bed and my handsome forty-three-year-old husband, lying there beside me was divine. God was so good. He had blessed us with comfortable living on a large grass seed farm, a perfect place to raise our three sons whom He had given us. Mark was 22, Lonnie would be 20 that next day, and Rob, our youngest, was 14. How I would have liked to just stay here in the comfort of his arms, but the activities of the day raced through my mind and I knew I must come to grips with reality. Willard smiled at me and said good morning. Then he answered the phone. After he got off the phone he lay back on the bed and said, "You know, Hon, I don't feel so well." So like we did many times, we stopped and asked Jesus to please make him feel better. We both hated to be sick. God truly had blessed us both with good health. We were so grateful for it.

The morning sped on as I got up and went about my usual Saturday tasks and before long Willard got up also. But he stretched out on the couch still not feeling very well. I went to him with some Seven-Up™ and then went back to my tasks of cleaning. Soon I realized he really didn't feel well at all. I thought it was the flu coming on, so I set on a pot of chicken soup and continued to check on him as I went about my weekend cleaning routine. How I loved to take care of him. It was so a part of my love for him, and the love I received back was so fulfilling.

As I worked, my mind was only half on my chores. My thoughts flitted to Willard, but I knew he'd be all right with a little rest and tender, loving care. I thought about the life we'd built here in western Oregon: a 2,500 acre grass seed farm that sold to clients all over the world, a successful manufacturing firm, and the house we'd designed and built ourselves.

When the soup was hot, I carefully carried it into the den. The room was so him, a Marlin fish he caught in Mexico hung on the wall behind him. The pretty wood ducks he had shot were mounted on the fireplace. The room felt so warm and homey. It held so many wonderful memories. They were sweet memories of our little boys growing up right here in this room—all the books we had read together, the games we had played with the boys. Many dreams were talked about in this room. Friends and their children had spent many happy hours here.

I hesitated in the doorway. There was Willard, still lying on the sofa—only this time there was a strange look in those wonderful eyes I loved so much. "Honey?" "Oh!" he said, suddenly pressing his hands to his chest. "It hurts." Then his eyes closed and his head fell gently back. There is no way to say exactly how intuitions come, but in the moment it took to set down the bowl and rush to Willard's side, I knew he was gone. I called to our youngest son, Rob, who had been playing table tennis with a friend in the family room. He rushed to call a neighbor and an ambulance. I sat on the sofa, cradling my husband's head in my arms. My whole life flashed before me. What would I ever do with out this man I loved so much. I prayed so hard, "Please, Lord, *please Lord*, don't let this be real." How can I help him? What can I do? Would help please come quickly! My anxious eyes met Rob's. I knew that he too was thinking, "How could this be happening to Dad?"

Minutes later, the ambulance arrived and a team of emergency medical technicians tried to revive him. One of the men who was specially trained in cardiac emergencies said it appeared that an aneurysm had burst in a major blood vessel near his heart. There had been no chance to save him. In an instant's time, my husband was gone. As I sat there, my sad eyes filled with fear and many tears. Fears of how could I go on alone. Thoughts of our older sons not being there flooded my mind. Would they think I had done all I could? How would my sons ever make it without their dad? What would I do? What could I do? I felt so helpless.

As the day went on I felt like a zombie. At times I didn't even feel that I was there. I had so many decisions to make. People came and went. There was nothing to do, but to ~~except~~ *accept* the awful truth. What meaning did life have now? What would tomorrow hold? My heart ached so much. As I watched my young sons, it felt like my heart would break. It was so unfair. Willard was such a great dad; how could I ever be a single parent? Rob was so young. He needed his dad so badly. I prayed that day, "Father, please be near my boys and comfort them." In the weeks that followed, it seemed as though I hardly existed. I tried to be strong for my sons, but they ended up being stronger for me.

How well I remember that first awful night, as we tried to just make it through. Mark got out his guitar and played songs of comfort to us. What a balm music was and would be to us during that healing time.

During this difficult time I held onto the good memories. But could I go on with only memories? I know we are not only promised bright tomorrows. After all, we live in a real world. Willard and I had lived each day as if it were our last day together. This had made my great loss much less full of regrets and the healing came much faster. There are many different dark tomorrows that we must face in this life. That is why it is so important that we love today for the inevitable dark tomorrow, whatever and whenever it may be.

No Regrets

The emotions that surged over me in the days after Willard's death were amazing in some ways. The most overwhelming feeling, of course, was the pain. Over and over I prayed, "Please, God, it can't be true. He was so young. I loved him so much." Why had this happened? Everything seemed to be going so well. I remember sitting for hours on our love seat just thinking and wondering what to do next. I was so blessed to have so many friends and family around me. Their love was so present. But nothing seemed to help the awful pain in my broken heart. I was so lonely. I longed to see his pick-up truck drive up, but it never did. Or to see that wonderful smile in those eyes I loved so much. But it wasn't there. Those first few weeks were just awful. I hardly remember anything but the pain that burned in my heart. But right in the midst of that pain was another feeling, a certain brightness of hope within. I can best explain it as a lack of regret.

One day, not long after Willard had left us, I was feeling very low. My son, Rob, was with me, and I began to cry. "If only I'd been with him all that morning," I said, "just sitting with him, instead of cleaning the house."

"Mom," Rob replied, "that one day was not nearly as important to Dad as all the other days and years he knew you loved him."

Rob's words reminded me, assured me, of Willard's love for me. I truly had little to regret about our twenty-four years together. And, just as important to me, our children had little to regret about their mom and dad's marriage.

When you love, it fills your life with security and beauty. It spills over into others around you—your children, family, and friends. The apostle Paul was certainly led of the Spirit when he wrote, "Love never fails" (1 Cor. 13:8 NEW AMERICAN STANDARD BIBLE). To put it another way, love overflows and goes on and on, blessing everyone it touches.

Try to live so the regrets are few. We can never go back. But if you have lost someone dear and are living with some deep regrets, ask Jesus to come into those hurts and heal the wounds left there. He can heal and restore.

Chapter Two

Expectations

can still recall those first feelings of being in love. In fact, I remember gazing happily out the window of the office where I'd started my first job as a bookkeeper. It was a vibrant November day, and I'd just told my handsome young farmer that I would marry him. It seemed as if all my dreams were coming true.

For years, I'd wanted to be married to a minister or to a farmer. Now I'd found a man who loved the land, had a good "business head," and was a strong Christian. He seemed so solid in his beliefs. Willard didn't really talk about his faith like the other young men I'd dated, but I was sure that would change. After we're married, I thought, I'll just make a suggestion here and drop a hint there. I'll make some "alterations."

Our wedding ceremony was beautiful; it went exactly as I had planned it. But after the wedding, my plan to make some alterations in Willard did not work at all. And, goodness knows, I tried.

Trying to Change Him

For instance, I really wanted Willard to carry his Bible. I thought that if he didn't want to talk about his faith, at least he could show it with some outward sign. Other young men I'd dated had carried their big, black leather Bibles. I knew Willard had a genuine respect for God's Word, but I thought he should show it a little more. In my immaturity, I thought carrying a Bible was a sign of spirituality.

At first I dropped hints, like putting his Bible out on the table before church. All my hints were unsuccessful. In fact, the more I hinted and the more persistent I became, the further it drove him from carrying his Bible. I knew Willard loved me. Why was he resisting in this one little thing?

For many years, I tried this same method of making "suggestions" about other things as well. I thought that if I kept making suggestions, maybe Willard would eventually do things the way I thought best. But again and again, I found my suggestions didn't bring about the change I wanted.

Then one day, years after we were married, we heard about some special, spiritual-life meetings to be held at a nearby church. We knew and liked the speaker. Even though we often went to meetings of this kind, I somehow felt these meetings would be important for us. Yet when I suggested we go, Willard did not immediately say yes.

The morning of the first meeting, I was about to open my mouth and suggest that I make supper early so we could be on time for the church meeting, but something inside stopped me. I thought, *This time I want to know that it's Willard's choice, not my prodding that's behind his decision. If he doesn't want to go, or if he comes in tired from the fields, we'll just stay home.*

All that morning I <u>simply prayed</u>. The feeling that these meetings were important did not go away, and I struggled with wanting to drop strong hints. But, no, I decided I would not do that this time.

About noon, Willard came in for lunch. To my great surprise he said, "Hon, I've been thinking about the meetings tonight. Let's plan to go." I was thrilled, of course, but still kept quiet.

At suppertime, the boys seem especially fussy. We had two little ones then, and it had been a tiring day with them. Now I was worn out. It would have been much easier to stay home. But I got the boys together, and off we went. Why was it so important to me for us to be at this meeting?

We arrived on time, and it proved to be a good service. But when it was over, I couldn't see why I'd felt it was so urgent for us to be there. It was only later, after we'd driven home and carried our sleeping boys to their beds, that it became clear.

Lying in bed that night, I was happy with the feeling of Willard's warmth beside me. After a few minutes, he said quietly, "I've decided to rededicate my life to Jesus. I want to give everything over to Him." My heart leapt. I gave him a tight hug and tears of joy filled my eyes.

I knew then why it had been so important for us to be at church that night. And another thought occurred to me. I suddenly knew why it was so important that I not suggest and hint that Willard take us. If I had done that, Willard might have resisted me and not been in the right place for the Holy Spirit to convict him of his need for a closer walk with the Lord.

Willard never did carry his Bible to church, though his spiritual life changed drastically. In terms of public ministry, he joined a gospel quartet, which eventually became a family-oriented ministry.

Shortly after the group started, their ministry expanded. Not only did they perform regularly in our church, but others also heard about the special sound these four men could produce and about the powerful testimony they gave in their music. Before long, they were singing in other churches in the area.

Eventually, this quartet grew and drew in the families of each of the men involved. Soon we were known as the Good Shepherd Quartet and Families. Our own children were still little when we began. But as they grew, they and some of the other children formed a back-up band for the singers. For eighteen years we traveled to churches all over the Northwest, encouraging others to serve the Lord.

This ministry truly was used by God to enhance our lives. The time together was so good for our family. Not only did it give us time together each weekend, but it also gave new meaning to our lives. For my sons, it helped them learn to be in front of an audience, and it developed their musical skills, skills that in their adult life would be helpful in their walk with the Lord. What a joy this group was to our family! It frightens me to look at this memory and realize had I not let the Lord do His work that night in Willard's heart, we might have missed all those wonderful blessings. Not only did my sons benefit, it was wonderful in Willard's life, too. Because Willard was shy, getting up and giving his testimony was something he longed to do but was difficult for him. Getting up and singing gave him the opportunity. God had blessed him with a wonderful bass voice. How wonderful it is if we just allow God to do His work, to lay down our expectations and allow His will for our lives.

Don't put your mate in a box and try so hard to conform him to that image. Jesus showed me that one of the strong points I loved so much in Willard was the way he believed something and lived it. There was not a fake bone in his body. I really did want him to be himself. It is sad, but often when our mates change to conform to how we "think" we want them, we do not like them that way after all.

When I was willing to respect Willard, I allowed God to do much more than I could have ever dreamed possible in both him and in our relationship. At home, he became more open in sharing his thoughts with me. We even began to read the Bible together.

A New Perspective

Through the experience that night at the special church service, God taught me an important lesson about the expectations wives have of their husbands. It took me a long time to see that even before Willard committed his life totally to the Lord, he was the spiritual head of our home. He had such integrity. It was more than human pride; he believed in righteous living. He loved to give generously and in secret. He carefully chose where he would give our money so that it would be used wisely to the most benefit. As a father, he loved the boys and disciplined them firmly, but fairly. And he loved me.

The funny thing was that once I saw more outward signs of his faith, I realized how deeply spiritual he'd been all along. But because he hadn't lived up to certain standards I'd set, he wasn't "spiritual" enough in my eyes.

That realization made me feel terrible. But there was something else that made me ashamed. All those years I'd dropped hints—and sometimes they were stronger than hints—I had actually driven Willard further away from the goal I really wanted!

When I stopped to ask God why I'd been that way, and why so many women I know badger their husbands, a verse came to mind: "For man looks on the outward appearance, but the Lord looks on the heart" (1 Sam. 16:7 AMPLIFIED). I had assumed I knew what was going on in Willard's heart between him and the Lord, but I'd been wrong.

Because I'd reacted to the outward "evidence" of Willard's faith, I'd been blind to other signs of his spirituality. So, fearing my husband wasn't spiritual, I prodded him with my helpful hints. The only result was that I caused him to react against *me*, and thus I undermined my whole plan. We can be so unaware of the harmful effects of our subtle pressure.

You may object immediately and say, "But I'm gentle in the things I suggest. My husband knows I love him, and I don't think I nag. Isn't he just being stubborn when he won't do something he knows I want?"

Many women struggle with these questions, because they don't know how men are motivated. A woman wants to be loved. She wants to feel she has a secure position at the center of a man's affections. A man also wants to be loved, but even more than that, he wants to be respected.

Once you understand this basic difference, you'll see how a nagging wife or even a wife who drops subtle hints can be hurting her relationship with her husband. In my case, I thought I was offering simple suggestions, wanting Willard to do certain things that would help him spiritually. But that wasn't all I was doing. My hints were saying to him, "I don't accept you the way you are. You have to do the things I want in order to be a better Christian in my eyes."

My focus was wrong. If you hold a coin in your fingers at arm's length, it looks small. You can clearly see other objects in the room around you. In fact, you might become interested in looking at something else and hardly notice the coin. But if you hold that coin up close to your eye, focusing on it intently, everything else in the room is concealed from your view. All you can see is the coin.

It's the same way for a woman who focuses in on one of her husband's flaws. Perhaps he's not making the kind of income she thinks he could, so she says he's lazy. He may be a good father and love his children. He may be a Christian with a heart that is fast after God. But because she's focused only on their financial struggle, she thinks of him as lazy.

Then the pressure begins. She comments casually, "It sure would be nice to be able to buy new furniture for the living room." Or, "Every boy on the baseball team has a new glove, but I guess we can't afford to buy Junior one, can we, dear?"

While some men may give in to this kind of pressure, most will fight against it inwardly. It is not in their nature to be controlled by a wife's critical, non-accepting spirit. In fact, a husband may have one of several responses. He may become angry and resentful and pull away from his wife. He may simply look for affirmation elsewhere, either in his work or among male companions. In the worst case, a man may even turn to another woman. But the result is the same—a wedge is driven between them.

The Need for Respect

Am I saying that a woman has no power or influence in a marriage? Quite the opposite! Where a man has final authority, I believe a woman has final influence in the home. As you can see by the examples I've used, and by my own mistakes, a woman has powerful impact. If she doesn't know that, or if she misuses it, she can bring great difficulties into her home. On the other hand, if she uses her influence wisely, she will bless her husband and her household.

I contend neither authority nor influence is better. Often when I am talking to women about this issue, their comment to me is, "My husband doesn't listen to me." My answer to them is, "Be in the Word every day. Spend time with the Lord daily. Then your husband will be able to trust your influence." If you are truly a woman of God, your husband will be foolish not to listen to your influence. On the other hand, if your husband is truly a man of God, it will be easier to give him the authority God has given him. A wise woman allows her husband to have final authority. Someone must have that final word. "A house divided against itself cannot stand." A wise man will listen to his wife's influence.

Women do seem to have a sixth sense. This sixth sense seems to have extra-sensory perception—a kind of inexplicable ability to understand circumstances and situations without being able to explain it in a reasonable way. For example, I heard a man once tell this story: He was putting together a business deal with a certain gentleman. The business plan that was laid out all seemed in good order. Like a wise man, he went to his wife and asked the businessman to show her the plan and tell her his proposal. His daughter was also there at the time of the presentation. After the businessman left, the husband asked his wife what she thought of the plan. She said the plan looked okay but the man was a snake. "A snake," the husband replied. "How can you say that when you hardly know him?" Her reply to her husband was, "I don't know; but he is a snake." Frustrated, he looked to his adult daughter and asked, "What do you think, honey?" She replied, "Daddy, he is a snake." The man went on to tell me, "I could not see how they could know, but he was a snake and ended up costing me a lot of money and heartache." Not always are we right as women, but often we have that sixth sense and our men would be wise to listen to it.

Notice even the little ways your husband hears you. When Willard and I were building our home, he wanted a brick fireplace and I wanted a stone one. After a few days of back and forth, Willard came home one day and said, "Hey, honey, how about a stone-faced fireplace?" That was a small thing, but it is so important that we notice those small times they listen. Be sure and tell him how much that blesses you. It will truly bless him and encourage him to listen more often to your influence.

The key is gaining an understanding of what it means to respect your mate. In Ephesians 5, husbands are told to love their wives, and wives are told to respect their husbands. When you are critical, flaw picking, and non-accepting, you are not respecting your husband. You are focusing only on his weaknesses, not on his good points. In an unspoken way, you are treating him like a child who needs to be corrected.

I believe that most adult men, when they do something wrong, they are aware it's wrong. Normally, you don't have to point out their mistakes. When you do, a man will build up a resistance to you, and your point is lost. Or worse, the atmosphere of non-acceptance will crescendo into an open fight.

On the other hand, when a wife responds positively to her husband, respecting him and complimenting his good points, something clicks on inside him. When a woman shows that she respects and trusts her husband, he wants to live up to that trust and respect. He is greatly motivated to be even more of a man after God's design.

When this kind of support begins to work in a marriage, you will stop the flow of negative forces at work between you, and you will spur each other on with a positive, upbuilding power. Yes, as women we can have godly influence in our homes. Proverbs 12:18 says, "There is one who speaks rashly like the thrusts of a sword, But the tongue of the wise brings healing" (NASB). Also, James says, in verse 3:5, "So also the tongue is a small part of the body, and yet it boasts of great things. Behold, how great a forest is set aflame by such a small fire!" (NASB) Our tongues have a great deal of power.

I'm not just talking about what we say verbally. Our inner attitude must constantly be directed toward building up our husbands, because what we do—even the slightest look—can express feelings, thoughts, and judgments.

If you try to change your husband, it says to him that you do not accept him as he is, and this makes his love for you diminish. Love grows out of the very climate of acceptance. Non-acceptance breaks communication and builds up tension. Let the change be up to God. He is so much wiser. His ways are not our ways. Don't take it into your own hands. He does work miracles. It is so easy to nag. It seems to be that when we nag, it is a sure sign we are not praying. Remember, prayer changes things. We do not fully understand the power of prayer. I have found that God does a much better job than I could ever do. He is so wise and really does want the best for us and our mate. Trust Him with your mate. It is easy to say we do trust Him, but not so easy to work it out. But if He does not bring about the change you hope for, then ask Him for grace and acceptance and understanding. So often God wants to work in our mate's life, and He can't because we are standing in the way.

I was talking recently with a young woman who was having trouble accepting some things about her husband. They were having minor disagreements, nothing overwhelming, but still she wanted a better marriage.

She began to practice some of the points in this chapter, and she stopped making comments aimed at "redirecting" him. She focused inwardly on his good points. Actually, she said very little to him.

Several weeks after she had made this conscious choice to change her way of thinking about her husband, he confronted her one day. "What's going on?" he demanded, smiling. "Why do you suddenly seem to love me so much? It's as if we're on a second honeymoon. I don't know what I'm doing right these days, but I wish you'd tell me!"

Think for a moment, what do you really think of your husband? Does he live up to your expectations? Have you been trying to alter him? Have you tried to use subtle pressures and hints?

Start thinking now about his good points. Tell him about them. Make it a priority to tell him what you respect about him. Give him the freedom to be himself. Cheer him in his progress.

Even if you already have a good marriage, you will see improvements you never dreamed possible. You'll find that, as hard as you root for your mate, he'll be rooting for you, too. You'll feel as if your marriage is beginning all over again.

Even if God doesn't work miraculous changes in your husband right away, He will continue to give you the grace to accept and understand. Some husbands are hard to love. But God values them nonetheless. As wives we must give God the freedom and time to work in our husbands' lives. When we stop complaining and start praying and loving, we are loosing God's Spirit to work in powerful ways.

When we love and accept things we do not like about each other, it no longer seems important. Often, if our husband feels loved and accepted, he will, on his own, try to change things he knows you do not like. Give him space, try not to focus on what you don't like and spend more time focusing on the things you love about him.

Sometimes we find that it is not our mate at all that needs to change, but us. Change is hard. Change is something we do not like to do. I am reminded that in a state of rapid change, our experience is our own worst enemy. We do not like change because it takes us out of our comfort zone. But change is good. We need to examine our hearts and make sure the change we want so much in our mate, really isn't a change needed in our life instead. It is so easy to see how our mate should change and so hard to see what change we should make. "First remove the plank from your own eye, and then you will see clearly to remove the speck from your brother's [husband's] eye" (Matt. 7:5 NKJV). It may sound silly, but Jesus used this example to emphasize how important it is that we do not judge or try to change the other person, because more than likely there is something bigger and more obtrusive in our own life.

I know in my life, change is hard. Laying down the way I saw things and accepting the way my husband saw things was often better. This is God's design for us, to learn from each other and not always need to be right. Lay down this strong desire to always have it your way.

In our life as husband and wife, we often perceive things quite differently. During the first years of my marriage, I perceived that when my husband saw things differently than I, he was probably wrong. Then I came to the realization that it was not so much who was right or wrong, but that we perceived things differently.

Once we overcome our wrong expectations, we can experience a deeper level of marriage. It is the greatest blessing God has for us as husband and wife. I am speaking of becoming one in Christ.

Chapter Three

Becoming One

What would bring the most fulfillment to your marriage? Having children? Establishing a family business? Building your "dream home"?

Often we replace the single most important goal in marriage, the thing essential to fulfillment in the relationship, with wrong goals. Becoming one with your husband will bring the most fulfillment. God intends for a husband and wife to become one. Genesis 2:24 says, "A man shall leave his father and mother and be joined to his wife, and they shall become one flesh" (NKJV).

One flesh! There are miracles in that phrase, in that unfathomable concept! What does it mean to be "one flesh"? In my mind's eye, I see myself lying beside Willard in his arms, feeling so at one with him. Years of living and loving together just bring that wonderful feeling of being one. It amazes me sometimes when two people live together for a long time, they sometimes begin to look alike. This wonderful feeling of being one is like blending together. Together, yet separate. The cord of love binds us together. It is one mystery that can not really be explained, but it is very real.

Today, unfortunately, a heavy emphasis is placed on independence. This independent attitude is the very thing that is destroying so many marriages. Why did God institute marriage at all? Because two people coming together in unity, can accomplish so much more together than either could accomplish alone. And in that unity, God demonstrates Himself to the world.

I found tremendous fulfillment in learning to work as a single unit with my husband. Willard was great at long-range planning, and I loved to help work out the details needed to reach those goals. But the responsibility for decision making was his, and that left me feeling liberated under his protection.

A good example of how we complemented each other while working together is the company we formed in 1980, Smucker Manufacturing. It all started when Willard saw something at an agriculture show in California, which gave him the idea for our first product—a more efficient way to apply weed killer to farm crops. Willard was great at seeing the potential in an idea and making it practical. I, on the other hand, with my orientation toward details, served as the travel agent, researcher, accountant, and executive secretary. Together, we built a thriving business.

How do you build *oneness* between you and your husband? This mystery is hard for our human minds to understand. The oneness that comes from intimacy between a husband and wife is the closest thing to heaven we have here on earth.

Many of us come into a relationship and immediately set boundaries and limitations. We say, "I'll do this, but only if you promise to do that." We want to have tight control over relationships, and the underlying reason is *fear*. We fear we will be taken advantage of or used. And when we fear, we cannot love freely. 1 John 4:18 says, "There is no fear in love, but perfect love casts out fear. For fear has to do with punishment, and he who fears is not perfected in love" (NEW REVISED STANDARD VERSION).

It is hard to reach out in love when we have been hurt. Often it is that hurt that brings the fear, fear of being hurt again. So rather than asking Jesus to heal us of that hurt, we let it fester and develop into fear. If you find yourself having a hard time loving and reaching out to your mate, get some advice based on the Bible from your pastor or a Christian counselor.

Becoming a Servant

The first step in becoming one with your husband is to take on the attitude of a servant. Philippians 2:2 says, "...being like-minded, having the same love, being one in spirit and purpose" (NIV). That means you are to love your husband as you would love yourself, to do for him what you would want done for you. Selfishness disrupts unity and destroys happiness. If you want to love as a servant, you cannot take the position that it's your husband's responsibility to make you happy. Instead, take the position that you are responsible for your own happiness. An attitude can be greatly improved by taking on a servant's attitude and realizing it is more blessed to give than to receive. Luke 6:38 says, "Give, and it will be given to you" (NIV).

In Luke chapter 6, we read about not picking on people, not looking for their failures, and not criticizing their faults unless, of course, you want the same treatment. We should not condemn those who are down. Be easy on people and you'll find your mate giving back, and not merely giving back, but giving back with bonus and blessing. Generosity begets generosity. How it would improve our marriages if we would follow these guidelines! When you give to someone, he can't help but give back to you. That's the beauty of taking on the attitude of a servant. To have a servant's heart is becoming more excited about seeing others fulfilled than yourself.

The Challenge of Submission

Another position you must take if you want unity and happiness with your husband is to *submit to his authority*. I realize many women today get upset when they hear these words. Unfortunately, submission has not been properly understood. In contemporary usage, to be in submission implies *inferiority*. This usage bears little resemblance, however, to the biblical meaning of the word. The biblical meaning of submission is not inferior at all. It states that there are different roles for men and women.

Even among Christians, the concept has been misunderstood and wrongly applied. Consequently, many Christian women have felt justified in disobeying God on this principle.

Nonetheless, submission is a biblical principle, and its proper application is another step in building true unity in marriage. Ephesians 5:21-22 says, "Be subject to one another out of reverence for Christ, the Messiah, the Anointed One. Wives, be subject—be submissive and adapt yourselves—to your own husbands as [a service] to the Lord" (AMPLIFIED).

The first thing to note about this passage is that it is honoring to Christ when we submit to our husbands. This is emphasized by the apostle Paul's statement, "Wives, submit to your own husbands, as is fitting in the Lord" (Col. 3:18 NKJV). The next verse says, "Husbands, love your wives and do not be bitter toward them." We each have our roles. God has spelled them out to us. Wives have the responsibility to revere their husbands so that their husbands are better able to love them.

One of the best concepts God has shown me is this: When we are perfectly content being submissive to our husbands, we discover that submission to his authority over us connects us to him. It interweaves and unites us together. In this same way, when our husbands are in submission to the heavenly Father, it unites him to the Lord and connects him with the Lord. With this concept, submission brings on a whole new meaning. We all desire to be better connected to our heavenly Father.

We must not come into every situation knowing how it must come out, because that is a controlling attitude, which is not submission. We all want to control in our different ways. Be careful of a controlling spirit. And remember that we all have our "special" ways of controlling.

Second, we recognize that God has ordained a certain family structure. In every organization there must be a president or a leader who makes the decisions; otherwise, there will be endless disputes. God gave this final authority to men, not that they should belittle women or ignore their thoughts and feelings, but that there should be order. With the final authority resting on them comes a great deal of responsibility for men. As the leader of the home, God advises them to heed godly counsel. By giving woman to man, God not only gave man a companion, but He gave him a helpmate, an advisor. Here the responsibility moves to the woman. As a helpmate, God commands woman to be in the Word and in tune with Him. Not only is this good for her personal walk with the Lord, but because she is in His word and in communication with Him, she is better equipped to support her husband and offer advice when requested. Being in the Word also puts her in the position where her husband can more readily listen to her counsel and trust her influence.

In this position of submission, the wife has ample room for expressing her feelings, hopes and desires, and for helping her husband think through a plan of action on any given issue.

Feminists often say the Bible gives men permission to run roughshod over their wives or even mistreat them. But men are to *love* their wives. Do you realize what love Jesus is talking about here? He said this love is the same love with which Christ loves the church. Wow, this is the love that caused Him to lay down His life for it. It is the love that is a deep and abiding concern for the welfare at all times of a man for his wife. The Bible does not say or even imply that a man should treat his wife as though she were mentally inferior. When it comes time to make the final decision, however, it must be left up to the man. This is the order God has chosen. And we know that God's ways are far better than our ways. If we live according to His ways, we will truly become one and our love for each other will be of the greatest possible kind.

In my own life I can think of some different times when my submission to Willard paid off. My mind goes back to the day Willard died. I had planned to spend the day with my friend. Earlier that week Willard said to me, "Hon, I really would like for you to call Sandy and tell her you can't help her on Saturday. Saturday is our day, and I really would like to spend it together." Little did I realize when I made that choice to submit to his wishes, how that would have such ramifications in my life. I can only imagine what consequences I would have suffered had I not heeded his request.

When a woman wrests the position of final authority from her husband in any way, she is bringing destruction upon her own home. She can do it in numerous ways. She can belittle him and his choices in front of his friends, colleagues, or even worse, his own children. She can allow him to think she's going along with him and then turn around and handle things her own way.

Each of these approaches shows rebellion, and each brings confusion and disruption into a home. This independent attitude quickly destroys unity, communication, and love. Women who undercut their husbands don't realize the far-reaching effects of their actions. In our family business, we employed many men as day laborers. Again and again, we saw the influence a wife had on her husband, for better and for worse.

When I think of women who support their husbands, I immediately think of the wives of two men who work for us. Sheila is always lively and on top of things, encouraging her husband, Ben, every step of the way. And there is Dot, who trusts the decisions of her husband, Walter, and stands behind him always. There is an enormous difference in the workplace between men like Ben and Walter and some others who worked for us in the past. These men are happy and have peace and confidence because they are built up and supported at home.

Giving God the Front Seat

A third position we must take if we want spiritual oneness with our husbands is to trust God. When we become tense and upset about something our husbands are doing or failing to do, we're really showing a lack of faith in God. Sometimes—even much of the time—we must relinquish our husbands into God's hands. Surely we can trust our heavenly Father to work out a plan that is best, not only for our husbands, but also for us. Jeremiah 29:11 says, "For I know the plans I have for you," declares the Lord, "plans to prosper and not to harm you, plans to give you hope and a future" (NIV).

As I said earlier, as a young woman I thought there could be nothing greater than to marry a farmer or a minister. Well, I got my farmer, but the part about the minister didn't come with the package—at least not right away. God had some work to do in Willard, and I had to learn how to walk by faith and not by sight (2 Cor. 5:7).

When we were first married, I wanted to attend a certain church in our area. Willard wasn't ready to make a change, so he wouldn't budge. I kept hinting that we try it out, but eventually (for once!) I felt I should leave it up to God to work in Willard's heart. After all, at least I had a husband who wanted to go to church.

After we'd been married about six years, Willard came to me one day and said, "I feel that God is leading me to take our family to a different church." And guess which one he suggested! If I thought that was the answer to my prayers, however, I was in for a bigger surprise.

Soon after we became established in our new church home, Willard was invited to sing with the group that I spoke of earlier. Being a part of the Good Shepherd Quartet and Families was an unforgettable experience for us all. It molded our sons in the service of the Lord and gave them spiritual insights at an early age into the needs of people. So my dream of having a farmer who was a minister came true, as I relinquished my plans to the Lord. More than that, our whole family was blessed as we grew in faith together. And through it all, Willard and I grew into a deep unity as husband and wife.

Isn't it interesting that I was looking for a minister who stood up and spoke eloquently? But in God's timing He had a much better plan. He gave me a man that ministered in song. Singing had always been a love of mine. Why is it so hard for us to learn that His ways are so much better then ours?

I sometimes shudder to think what would have happened if I had begged and pleaded and nagged Willard about taking me to the church where I wanted to go before he was ready. Of course, I know things don't always turn out exactly as we hope, and I can't promise you the fulfillment of every one of your desires, for not all of mine have been fulfilled. But I do know that God desires for husbands and wives to become "one flesh." And sometimes this means letting go of our dreams in order to let God fulfill them in His way and in His timing. Along the way, as was the case in our home, I know He will answer your prayers beyond your wildest imaginings.

It is no small thing that Proverbs, the greatest book of wisdom on earth, closes with words of praise for the godly woman. She works constantly to serve her husband, to submit to him, and she constantly relinquishes him in prayer to God. In the words of Solomon, "Charm is deceitful, and beauty is vain, But a woman who fears the LORD, she shall be praised. Give her a share in the fruit of her hands, and let her works praise her in the city gates" (Prov. 31:30-31 NRSV).

When a woman gives herself to her husband, first in service and then in submission, a transformation will take place in her marriage. The woman who chooses this path to unity with her husband need not fear that she will be made to give and keep on giving while her husband takes no notice. For when a man senses this kind of unselfish love, when he feels the unqualified support of his wife, he will turn to her and say, "What can I do to bless you, to make you feel fulfilled?"

Conclusion

Submission is a theological term describing the authority relationship of Christian wives to their husbands. The usage of this word to the world bears little resemblance to the theological term. Satan uses the confusion of the two meanings of this word to persuade Christian wives to feel justified in disobeying God in this area. Remember, if you are submissive to your husband, you are more loveable and able to accept your husband's love. The world's usage of this word implies inferiority, but our wise and loving God had no such meaning in mind. Our roles complement each other if we allow them to. We are equal in soul, spirit, and mind and also in position, freedom, and happiness. I have learned that the more I submit, the more freedom he gives me. Enjoy being submissive and he will respond. Not out of duty, but willingly and with love. So much depends on our attitude.

No matter how much "in love" a couple may be when they are first wed, they are still two minds, two personalities, and two souls. It takes a lot of work and love to become one. But the rewards of unity are beyond compare. Then, when we have laid aside our independence and learned to walk in unity, we'll find that the man who walks at our side will become our greatest friend on earth.

Chapter Four

Making a Marriage Sparkle

Some women dream of keeping that special sparkle in their marriages forever. But most, I'm afraid, let go of that dream after the first couple of years of married life. "A sparkling marriage?" they retort. "Maybe for newly-weds. But after awhile—well, it's just unrealistic. The sparkle wears off for everyone."

Think for a moment about the early days of your marriage. If you were already home when he came in from work, can you recall the joy of his homecoming? Did you ever wake up before he did and just lie there, studying his face, loving to look at him? Willard and I were in love like this. And I can recall the moment, some years after we were married, when I first noticed that the sparkle had dimmed. It was a difficult day.

We were expecting guests for the weekend. I was getting clean sheets out of the linen closet—the "good linens" for the visitors. As I slid the sheets off the shelf, I had a sinking feeling. Gone was their pure white crispness. They looked washed out and limp. As I continued preparations for the weekend, I began to notice other signs of wear that I'd overlooked until then—a chip in the pretty rose china we'd been given as a wedding gift, a dent one of the boys had made in the wooden table top. Not that our possessions mattered so much to us, but their worn look called my attention to something far more important.

We were in our ninth year as husband and wife—nine happy, blessed years. We had added two healthy boys and a new home into our marriage. We loved each other. But I felt further apart from Willard than I had before we were married. We just didn't seem close anymore. Like the dull sheets and the chipped china, our marriage seemed to have lost its freshness.

Mentally, I took a half-panicked inventory. Had Willard changed? Had I? Had we taken each other for granted? Was our marriage going wrong? I hated the feeling that we had lost something forever; that it had slipped from our fingers without our notice.

We used to love to spend as much time together as possible. Even when Willard was working long hours on the combine during harvest season, I often rode with him. Of course, that changed when the boys came along. I needed to give them as much of my time as possible, I had reasoned.

In the days following my initial panic, I searched my heart and watched our relationship. I observed what we were like when we were with each other. It was awful. We could be in the same room, looking at one another, talking to each other—and I still had the terrible sense that we were not communicating. This was true even when the children weren't in the room, and we could talk without interruption. I felt that something inside me was not touching the inside of him. With that came the terrible doubts. Maybe we'd outgrown each other somehow. Maybe he felt it, too. We had even become haphazard about kissing good-bye in the morning when he left for work. And what if he had started to look elsewhere—to his work, to hobbies, or perhaps to someone else—for fulfillment that he used to find in being with me?

So we did what many people do when they feel their marriage needs rejuvenating—we had another baby!

Our third son, Rob, was an adorable baby. He won our hearts instantly. What's more, it was such fun to have a new baby again. And just as I'd hoped, things were better between Willard and me—for awhile.

In spite of our happiness with Rob, our marriage did not improve. Before long, we were back in the same rut, almost living separate lives under one roof. Are any of these feelings familiar? Whether you feel your marriage has lost its sparkle or is still shining brightly, I want to tell you what we learned about keeping the sparkle in our marriage.

Maintaining Togetherness

It was near our tenth anniversary, and I was still feeling unsettled and helpless. By this time, I knew Willard was as aware of the problem as I was. Then he made a decision that changed our marriage.

He came into the kitchen one evening, looking tired after a hard day in the fields. He would always hug me as though a ritual. This time he held me close in his arms and looked me in the eyes. "Hon, we need to get away together," he said with a smile. "Just you and me."

My first inward response was, Oh, no! What about our little boys? And the baby? They need me! How could my children survive without Mommy? "Why don't we take the kids with us?" I suggested.

Willard pulled away and his smile faded.

I could tell this meant a great deal to him. I knew that our marriage needed something. Even still, it took me some time to work through my feelings about leaving the boys in order to be alone with my husband. As a Christian parent, I'd been taught to devote a lot of time to my children. I loved my boys. How I wanted to be a good mother!

In the end, we left the boys in capable hands and took a short trip to San Francisco. We didn't have a lot of money to spend, but that didn't matter, because it was a major turning point in our marriage.

I can still recall the hilly streets with their cable cars, the romantic dinner overlooking the Bay and our walks along the piers. We were together, just the two of us—away from the distractions of the farm and the interruptions from the children. He was there all for me. I was there all for him. The entire trip was all about us. A change from the ordinary, since "us" was usually last on the priority list. We were together again in ways we had not been together in a long, long time.

This was the beginning of a new relationship. Everything didn't change overnight. It took lots of work and time. But a door opened, and we began to talk honestly with each other. Some things we said hurt, but the hurt was healthy, because it was wrapped in the solid commitment of our love.

How do you keep the sparkle in your marriage? The first thing we learned is this: Take time for one another. Even though you pass the time doing the same things—eating at the same table, sitting side-by-side on the sofa watching television, or sleeping in the same bed—it doesn't mean you are spending time together. In his book, *Connecting*, Larry Crabb says, "I have come to believe that the root of all our personal and emotional difficulties is a lack of togetherness, a failure to connect that keeps us from receiving life and prevents the life in us from spilling over into others. I therefore believe that the surest route to overcoming problems and becoming the people we were meant to be is reconnecting with God and with our community."[1] Connect with your mate. Let him know how much you care, just by being there for him.

When you have children, your time together drastically gets cut. Certainly, in the early months of a baby's life, mom's constant nurturing care is necessary. But too often, mothers continue to feel their children's total dependency long after it is necessary. I'm not suggesting you neglect your children. There is a time for that intense nurturing, but all along you must remember you are a wife, first and foremost. I am not speaking just of the physical relationship, but also of the time and attention it takes to keep a marriage alive. Don't feel guilty for taking time just for the two of you. There will be security in that for you as a couple, and also for your children.

We'll look more at the effects of a good marriage on children later. For now, I want to emphasize that becoming a mother doesn't mean you have to give up being a wife. One of the hurtful things I learned, as Willard and I began to communicate again, was that it seemed to him as though I'd stopped caring. He felt I was spending all my effort on the boys, and he was given whatever was left over. He was mostly right.

Not long ago, I heard this description of marriage on the radio broadcast, *Focus on the Family.*[2] When two people get married, it is like each of them getting in a boat, his and hers. They start out together at the shore of this lake of life. They go along for awhile together. Then, the storms hit and they start going different directions. Before long, she has gone to the south shore and he to the north shore. Not at all what they set out to do. The problem was perhaps they did not know how to work the oars, or maybe they did not want to put all the work it took into going the same direction. I think this is a great example of what often happens in marriages. It takes work to pull together. It takes communication and encouragement from each other. Decide today that it is worth the effort, so you can row side by side and not end up on opposite sides of the lake of life.

Special "I Love Yous"

You can communicate to your husband you care in lots of little ways, more than your actual words. It doesn't take a huge effort or a lot of time or money. It can mean fixing his favorite meal or surprising him with going out for a candlelit dinner. (A wife doesn't have to wait for her husband to ask her on a date, after all!) A small thing I did was to put little notes in Willard's lunch on occasion. You can be as creative as you'd like.

Once, around the time of Willard's birthday, I was trying to think of something special to give him. I didn't want to get him another tie or bottle of cologne. Then an idea came—I'm sure it was from the Lord, because I'm not that creative. I would get a simple inexpensive notebook, and each day from then until his next birthday, I'd write down something about him that made me love him!

For 365 days, I kept that love journal. What a joy it was to take time each day to turn to that little notebook! I have to be honest and say there were some days when I just couldn't find anything positive to write. Those days were few, fortunately, so I'd read what I'd written on one of the earlier days. This turned into a great blessing for me. And as the months passed and Willard's birthday approached, my anticipation grew.

I will never forget the look in Willard's eyes when he unwrapped my precious little book on his birthday. He chuckled at my honesty when I told him about the blanks. And he was greatly moved to read about himself as seen through my eyes.

Sometime later, after Willard had died, I was cleaning out some things and came across that little book I had given him all those years ago. I opened it, and through tears, read the things I had written. It brought comfort to me that day. Comfort that God had given me that special idea. My mind went back to that day I handed him this gift. What joy that little book brought to me to see the love in his eyes as he read the pages! That love brought comfort to my heart. You can never lose by loving.

A friend shared another idea with me. She purchased a heart-shaped bottle and filled it with notes describing what she loved about her husband. She did this at a time when she was having trouble thinking she really loved her man. She shared with me that this helped her realize he did have some good traits, and it helped her fall back in love with him. She said, that like me, it helped her to look in the jar at what she had put in on another day. It was especially helpful on days when she couldn't think of anything to put in the jar.

I am sure there are many other ways we can remind ourselves of how much we love our mate. The Lord loves to give us ideas on how to do just that. The hard part is listening, then following what He says.

For these ideas to be effective, effort is required. Whether your demonstration of love is elaborate or simple, it is most effective when it communicates that you are sensitive to your husband's needs, his likes, and dislikes. In this, I learned to watch for unspoken responses, as well as for spoken ones. I learned to pick up on small comments dropped in casual conversation and to watch his facial responses in order to read his moods. Willard was not a talker, so it wasn't always easy to know what was going on inside him.

Am I giving you the impression that effective communication with someone you love is hard work? Then you're reading me loud and clear! When you zero in on your husband's personality, interests, and needs, he can't help but be affected and return the consideration.

We must realize that marriage is the very top of all earthly relationships. It is the closest union of a man and woman in the sight of God. Because of this, marriage can be and should be the biggest contribution to your emotional health. But for this to be real in a marriage, you must value one another. God has made us to desire to be fulfilled through our relationship with our mate. We have the power to crush the spirit of our mate. I really think we wives don't realize the power we have over our husbands. And, as a matter of fact, that they have over us. God designed us to need each other. He put in us the desire to be loved and cared for by our mates. We need to respect them as it says in Ephesians 5:33, "So again I say, each man must love his wife as he loves himself, and the wife must respect her husband" (NEW LIVING TRANSLATION).

Philippians 2:2-3 says, "Fulfill my joy by being like-minded, having the same love, being of one accord, of one mind. Let nothing be done through selfish ambition or conceit, but in lowliness of mind let each esteem others better than himself" (NKJV). To keep the sparkle in your marriage, be sure to focus on the good points of your mate. It is very important for you to establish an attitude of acceptance. When you express to your mate your appreciation of his goodness, it helps to become aware of his strengths, and helps him feel better about himself. In turn, there will be more love between the two of you, and the sparkle will be brighter.

In Philippians 4:8 it says, "For the rest, brethren, whatever is true, whatever is worthy of reverence *and* is honorable *and* seemly, whatever is just, whatever is pure, whatever is lovely *and* lovable, whatever is kind *and* winsome *and* gracious, if there is virtue *and* excellence, if there is anything worthy of praise, think on *and* weigh *and* take account of these things—fix your minds on them" (AMPLIFIED). This is not to say we should stuff our feelings of hurt, but deal with them and then dwell on the good thoughts.

Building Trust

Another reason the sparkle can leave a marriage is that some men feel they cannot trust their wives. I don't mean they're suspicious, but they're concerned about trustworthiness in a way most women don't even consider.

It's difficult for many men to express their private thoughts and emotions. This is just the way some men are, and wishing it were otherwise won't change things. But when a man shares something intimate, he expects complete confidence. He wants to know you can be trusted. But sometimes when a husband talks about emotions, he senses that his wife is telling them to her best friend. There is a principle to remember here. When we break that trust with our mate, it is difficult to restore. Although difficult, it does not have to be impossible. It takes time to rebuild that trust. It is not easily restored. When we break that trust, we must be patient with our mate as we rebuild the trust we once had. In rebuilding trust, it takes more actions than words. If we can remember how hard it is to rebuild trust, we will be more careful not to break trust again, or in the first place.

This is true of many women. Unfortunately, it is most true of Christian women! Sometimes, as Christian women, we share intimate things about our spouses in prayer groups. We pick up the phone and call a close sister in the Lord. Or we may seek out our pastors. Not all of what is said should be shared. More than that, the more a woman relies on others to be her confidantes, the less she needs her husband's confidence.

So, if you want to see the luster stay in your marriage or return, be your husband's confidante. Be trustworthy with the feelings and secrets he has entrusted to you.

Don't Neglect the Physical

Yet another reason marriages lose their sparkle is that couples neglect their sexual relationship. While I want to address this issue I'm not going to get explicit with suggestions for helping your sex life. First, what works for one couple may not work for another. Second, it's so important for you to learn what pleases your man. And third, in this realm of intimacy, it will improve your communication greatly to learn about him from him. The sexual relationship is such an important part of marriage. But couples, especially those who have been together for years, can become dangerously neglectful of each other.

Let's talk a bit about intimacy. Intimacy is far more than the act itself. It is very different for men and for women. Great intimacy requires lots of communication between the husband and wife. Over the years, I can remember times when it was unfulfilling because we did not communicate. Willard and I were very different in the way we viewed things. I did not always know how to tell him what I was feeling, and this occasionally caused a roadblock between us. To a man, sex is so much what they see and it is immediate; there are not a lot of yesterdays in it. To a woman, it is what happened earlier that day or even many days before. We say men are like filing cabinets—so compartmental. When in the kitchen they want to do kitchen things, when in the bedroom they want to do bedroom things, with little thought about what just went on in the kitchen. Women are like streams. Women are so affected by what is put in upstream. We cannot have true fulfillment with any pollution coming down from upstream. So communicate with each other. Get the stream cleaned before you are intimate with each other. If we can remember how men are motivated and driven, it will help us. If our husbands can remember to keep our streams clean, it will help them.

When Willard and I had an argument as he was going out the door, it usually was left unresolved even after he came home. Then that evening, he would want to be intimate without working through what we were arguing about. I am not saying you can always come to an agreement. But women don't like to make love when there is an unresolved conflict that is stuffed away. "Stuffing" is a sure killer of fulfillment in intimacy with our mate. Try hard not to stuff it and communicate with your husband. Even if it hurts, it is so much better then stuffing. It leads to bitterness and lots of pollution in the stream. The most physically beautiful women who become bitter are soon quite unattractive. Bitterness has a way of rotting us from the core. Don't ever let bitterness set in. Learn to communicate with your mate.

Be open with your mate during your time of intimacy. Maybe you like to make love in the morning, because of your job and the responsibilities with your family. By evening you are just too tired. If your husband does not know this, he may think you are just being unresponsive to him. Until you communicate this to him, he has no way of knowing. This can be a very big deterrent to your time of intimacy.

Tell your partner what pleases you and ask him to share with you what pleases him. Be open and honest. Remember to stay current; things that please us change. My mood changes on a daily basis; what pleased me yesterday may not be what pleases me today. Keep current with your communication.

Sex is too important to marriage to assume it is merely a symptom that will take care of itself when other problems are solved. That is not true. Sex is a building block for constructing and maintaining a solid, happy marriage. A good sexual relationship can keep a marriage together when a lot of other things are shaky.

Closely related to the sexual aspect of marriage is physical appearance. Remember when you and your husband were first seeing each other? You probably went to great lengths to look appealing, primping and preening, trying to wear the most flattering clothes. Do you still hold that attitude, or are you neglectful of your appearance?

We need to look the best we can for our husbands. You need not spend lots of time each day, but take a few minutes to fix your hair, and put on a tasteful touch of makeup, and dress in clothes that are neat and becoming. It requires such little effort, really, and I guarantee your husband will appreciate it. You'll also feel better about yourself, and that will make you feel better about him, too.

You might even ask your husband to help you pick out your clothes. If he doesn't like to shop, you can always ask his opinion about the styles he likes to see you wear. You can show him pictures in a catalog or model your purchases for him.

Some women feel they have a right to look the way they want. They consider makeup and choice of clothing their business. I certainly had a mind of my own in all these matters, but it was important to me to know what Willard liked and to live up to his best picture of me. Because he saw that I tried to please him in this, it pleased him.

Showing Respect

Along with caring, trust, sexuality, and your appearance, there is one other crucial principle of marriage. It can break a relationship or make it shine. I am referring to the respect and admiration we show to our husbands. Ephesians 5:33 says, "Let the wife see that she respects *and* reverences her husband" (Amplified).

Admiration of your man is so essential to his happiness and fulfillment. It helps build his self-worth and self-confidence. Men love admiration from anyone, but it is ever so much more meaningful from the one they chose to love and marry. Proverbs 3:27 says, "Do not withhold good from those who deserve it" (NIV). When your husband deserves encouraging, loving words from you, don't hold back. Make it a practice to speak love and admiration in your home.

Another aspect of admiration that goes deeper than words is the way you think about your husband. It's important to establish an attitude of acceptance. In 1 Corinthians 13:4-5, Paul said, "Love...keeps no record of wrongs" (NIV). Some women keep long accounts of the irritating or hurtful things their husbands did, do, and probably will do. They become seething volcanoes of anger and resentment. When that anger has worked deep and long enough, it becomes depression.

It's obvious that any two people who live together are going to hurt and anger each other. That's the way life is. The secret of keeping an admiring spirit is to have a forgiving heart. The longer you store away moldy, old hurts and petty gripes, the more they will rot away your respect for your husband.

I learned to make a regular, spiritual housecleaning of my thoughts. This always re-established an attitude of admiration in me for my husband. Goethe, the German author, said, "If you treat a man as he is, he will stay as he is. But if you treat him as if he were what he ought to be and could be, he will become that bigger and better man." If you believe your man is a good husband, you will talk as if he's a good husband. Then you will treat him as if he's a good husband, and he will become a good husband. Affirmation and love unlock the door to a warm, sparkling marriage.

Just as you should think admiringly of your husband, a wife needs to act admiringly toward her husband. Some women today have an independent, I-don't-need-a-man's-help sort of attitude. But depending on your husband for help will appeal to his manly attributes. Fulfilling your husband is not denying him the fulfillment he feels by allowing him to protect you. If you want to be happier and more relaxed, restore in your husband a desire to care for you. Start with physical things. Let him carry the vacuum cleaner downstairs or move the furniture. Let him know you depend on him. When you feel yourself over-burdened and over-pushed, let your husband help you. He can't help you unless you let him know you need help. Seek his opinion and rely upon him as the final authority in your home. This attitude will appeal to something deep inside him that wants to shepherd and protect.

Just as admiration builds up your man, being put down, especially in front of someone, tears him down. We do so much damage when we belittle our mate. It is sad, but I have seen couples "get back " at their mate in front of others. Not only does this belittle the mate, but it is also embarrassing for the friends. Try very hard not to confront your mate when others are around. This is especially important in front of your children. We might think that if we embarrass our mate enough, he will think twice about doing "whatever" to us again. But in fact, it only makes him angry and feel like he now needs to get even with you. Often husbands feel defeated and think it is not worth trying. It is a vicious circle. Don't get caught in that trap.

Proverbs 18:21 says, "Death and life are in the power of the tongue" (NKJV). That means your words can bring life to your husband and marriage, or they can tear down and destroy both.

How do you apply this wise proverb? You don't have to be fawning and complimenting your man all the time. But consider this, do you fly off the handle and say terrible, destructive things when you're angry, or do you try to give a soft answer? A harsh reply will make him defensive; a soft reply will allow him to change his mind without being threatened. Do you belittle him when he's made a mistake or hurt you? Encouraging him to try again and telling him you know he can succeed, will make him strong. Do you take for granted the long hours he works to support the family? Thanking him will build up his spirit and self-esteem and can make his job seem more worthwhile, no matter how difficult it is. Does he only hear your complaints, or does he sometimes hear, "I'm glad I married you"?

Philippians 2:3 says, "With humility of mind let each of you regard one another as more important than himself"(NASB). To keep the sparkle in your marriage, be sure to focus on the good points of your mate.

Keep Praying

Spend time together in prayer. The sparkle will return when you pray together. There is something about the bonding that takes place when we pray together about things that are near and dear to our hearts. Nothing thrills me more then to hear my husband praying for our family or for the special concerns of his heart. It gives me a glimpse of what matters most to him, and it is really hard to be deceptive in prayer. What wonderful joy it brought to Willard and me when we would experience a direct answer to our prayer. When we wanted to build a new home, I remember Willard saying to me that if the next year's crop was extra good, we would build our home. As the time rolled on, we chose a particular field to use just for it. It was a clover field. Together, we sorted though all the seed, one by one, that we would plant in that field. Do you know how small clover seed is? It was an endless job. But it was so rewarding doing it together. Then it was planting time. How we prayed as we planted the seed. As you know, it takes time for seed to grow. Each time we passed that field we prayed. Then came harvest. It was a great harvest. Far greater then we could have ever hoped for. What a joy it was for us to see our prayers being answered before our eyes. That field brought in the necessary funds for us to build the home we so desired. It brought such unity and joy to us. Over the years as we enjoyed our lovely home together, we were continuously refreshed. Today, my oldest son and his wife are enjoying that home. Never underestimate what can happen when you bind your hearts together in prayer.

Man's answer to problems is to try to solve them on his own. Women, even Christian women, can get caught up in this same behavior when it comes to trying to handle marital problems. When our efforts fail and our husbands don't change, we become frustrated. Frustration usually leads to nagging. Proverbs 21:19 says, "It is better to live in a desert land than with a contentious and fretful wife" (NRSV). We don't like to hear that, but it's true.

We cannot solve marital frustrations on our own. God wants us to pray. Prayer does change things. Nagging (chapter 2) is a pretty good sign that you're not praying or that you're praying with wrong motives. We pray, "Oh, God, change this, that, and the other about my husband." God knows your husband's sins and flaws. That doesn't mean you shouldn't confess your hurts to God. But when you do, allow Him to heal them. And above that, what He wants you to pray for is mercy and blessing for your husband. In this kind of prayer, a wife is released from a nagging spirit. She can trust God to do what she cannot. Even the hardest heart can be softened through prayer.

Conclusion

I realize that some husbands are hard to love. So often today, women want to bail out of a difficult relationship before they have even tried to make it work. We must each realize that God loves our husbands so much more than we do or can. Your man is of infinite worth to God, just as you are. Knowing that God values your husband makes your efforts worthwhile.

When you practice the things discussed here, you will find that Philippians 2:2 becomes a reality in your marriage. Remember what the apostle Paul wrote, "Then make my joy complete by being like-minded, having the same love, being one in spirit and purpose" (NIV). What a joy to be two, yet one!

Begin today to rekindle the fires of godly love between you and your husband. Do away with the attitudes, sinful actions, and words that tarnish your relationship. With God's help, you can keep the sparkle in your marriage!

Chapter Five

Love and Friendship

Important as it is to keep the sparkle in your marriage, a wife can sometimes overlook an even more basic goal: Make your husband your best friend, and make yourself his best friend. Nothing could better describe the love we want to have for our husbands than these words from the apostle Paul:

> Love is patient and kind. Love is not jealous or boastful or proud or rude. Love does not demand its own way. Love is not irritable, and it keeps no record of when it has been wronged. It is never glad about injustice, but rejoices whenever the truth wins out. Love never gives up, never loses

faith, is always hopeful, and endures through every circum-
stance…There are three things that will endure—faith,
hope, and love—and the greatest of these is love.

1 Cor. 13: 4-8,13 NLT

Love is commitment, both to God and to a person. When we
make this commitment, we're saying, "I will give you true love.
And when I don't feel like it, I will give until I do feel like it."

Most Americans marry for love, but that word means nothing to them like the definition Paul gave it. To most contemporary Westerners, love equals sexual attraction and a warm
feeling inside. No wonder our media depicts love as something
beyond our control. It is here today and gone tomorrow. When
it's here, get married; when it's gone, get divorced.

What is real love? We often love others on a conditional
basis. Ours frequently is an "if-list" of love:

I will love you if your behavior meets my approval.
I will love you if you do as I say.
I will love you if you dress the way I want you to.
I will not love you if you disagree with me.

True love is much deeper than sexual attraction or romantic feelings. This love is true relationship, which grows out of
knowing your husband, being aware of his needs, and being
unselfish, giving, and caring. This love does not depend on feelings and it does not fade as your husband grows older; instead,
it deepens. It is a matter of choice, lodged in the will. Genuine
love grows from a deep understanding and appreciation for a
lasting relationship.

Even Christians who can recite 1 Corinthians 13 by heart
are still tainted by the world's brand of love. We often apply
Paul's words to complete strangers and yet forget to apply them

to those closest to us. I know I have had trouble with this. For instance, if Willard or one of the boys walked over a freshly waxed floor, I became upset. But if a neighbor boy accidentally walked in, my reaction was different. I might not even mention the fact that he was ruining my hard work. It is sad to me that we react so much faster to the ones we love best.

Working at Friendship in Marriage

Why don't we connect the two words work and love? True, committed love, the basis for a strong friendship, is work. You can fall into love (that is, infatuation), but you do not fall into friendship. You build friendship through shared experiences and through learning to trust. Friends share dreams and celebrate successes without being jealous. They are nonjudgmental, yet they can point out when you're making a fool of yourself. Friends enjoy the reward of a grateful smile. They relax with each other because of the atmosphere of sincere, unconditional acceptance.

As wonderful as this friendship with your man is, there is always risk involved. We have to put our hearts and emotions on the line. We become vulnerable. That's the nature of a close friendship. Close friendships are actually love relationships. We truly want to be in a close love relationship with our mate. This love relationship does not just happen. We never quit working on this wonderful love relationship with our mate. All good things are worth working for. Choose to be the best friend you can be to your mate. The reward of this great friendship is so very fulfilling. Friendship is risky, but it has more to gain than lose. It is worth the gamble.

In a marriage relationship we must be what I call a "servant friend" to our mate. To be a servant friend we must care deeply, unselfishly, and patiently, putting care into action. We must add more to our mate's life than take away from his life. We must affirm them, knowing that building up their self-esteem does not demerit our own.

Giving trust and deserving trust is also something we must do. When we have a servant friendship with our mate, we love them because of who they are and not for what they have or are going to have. A servant friend is love in action. We all need this in our lives. The best way to get your mate to be one with you is to be one with him. There is no limit to my potential for service to my husband if I allow God to work through me, in spite of me. John 15:13 says, "Greater love has no one than this, than to lay down one's life for his friends" (NKJV).

Isn't this the kind of friendship you want with your husband? Isn't it worth working for?

Larry Crabb, also in his recent book, *Connecting*, says, "It is time for the people of God to enter the primary battle we're all fighting, to connect with each other not about problems but about our desire to know God. The great danger, if we accept it, is that we will see how bloody the battle is and quickly distribute Band-Aids and aspirin."[1] I believe this, too, is so true in a marriage.

What is friendship really? I like to think of friends like jewelry. Some are like costume jewelry and some are like real gold and silver. Then there is the friend who is like a diamond, a rare gem too priceless to value. This is your best friend, your husband. Guard this diamond. Treasure this diamond. Take good care of it. There is no one more precious to you than this diamond. The greatest token of friendship is to feel utterly and totally welcome into another person's life. Are you this kind of friend to your husband? To be the best of friends you need to spend quality time with each other. How can you get to know each other, to love each other, and to be best of friends if you do not spend time getting to know what makes each other happy? Try to get away on a trip together.

The weekend to San Francisco with Willard was a great

example of just that. We became friends that weekend. You build a friendship through experience. Friends trust experience, even in the midst of our strengths and weaknesses.

Friends enjoy giving compliments just to see a grateful smile. My heart still does a little flip when I think how wonderful Willard's grateful smile made me feel.

Proverbs 17:17 says, "A friend loves at all times" (NKJV). Marriage is certainly the place where genuine friendship is necessary, maybe more than in any other friendship. It is not just necessary, but a "must" in a good marriage.

This precious bond of marriage and friendship is so fragile and therefore requires daily care. It deserves every ounce of your energy to make it grow. A good marriage begins with friendship. But friendship does not stop when love begins. That is the secret—friendship never stops.

The weekend Willard and I decided to become best friends, to start with a new effort, was the beginning of something wonderful. We did not become the best of friends overnight. I can't even put my finger on exactly when or how it all happened. That weekend, when we made the decision to start, we realized our friendship had changed. We felt taken over by a subtle, but deep sense of happiness and contentment. It is a contentment that can't be measured.

Alan Loy McGinnis in *The Friendship Factor* says, "Some of America's leading psychologists and therapists were asked how many men ever have real friends. The bleak replies were 'not nearly enough' and 'too few.' Most guessed that as few as ten percent of American males enjoy close friendships with anyone."[2] What a grim picture! With this sad statistic in mind, let me ask: Isn't it wise for a woman to take the initiative to cultivate friendship with her husband? If you make a concentrated effort to understand and meet the needs of your mate, I promise , you will find the dearest pal of your life. How do we build this lifelong kind of friendship that is so necessary to a wonderful marriage? Earlier, we talked briefly about giving attention to the things that interest your husband. Showing this kind of interest is one of the most important things you can do to build a foundation of love.

I can already hear some of you groaning! I know what you're thinking, "But I hate football! I don't enjoy talking about politics. Money matters and talk about investments don't interest me in the least."

I know exactly what you mean. One of the things my husband and sons most enjoyed on Sunday afternoons was going to fish hatcheries. Somehow that was not a turn-on for this wife and mother. I tried to reason with myself that they worked long, hard hours on the farm and deserved this enjoyment, and they had at least chosen an activity on which I could go along. But my inner response remained the same—fish hatcheries, no less!

I forced myself to go along grudgingly—until I realized the effect my unwillingness was having. I was dampening their joy and ruining my own Sunday afternoon. It was then I decided to change things. I brought along a book or some stationery so I could write a letter while Willard and the boys watched the fish. If the weather was nice, I'd bring a blanket and sunbathe.

It wasn't long before I began to enjoy our Sunday outings. And it became clear to me that the reason for my change of attitude was that I'd made a choice. I learned you can make almost anything pleasant or unpleasant depending on your attitude. I even came to enjoy not just trips to the hatcheries, but fishing trips as well.

I guess you've caught on that fishing was a big deal in our family. I really wanted to like to fish, but hard as I tried, I could never enjoy standing on a riverbank and swatting mosquitoes, while holding a pole with a dying worm on a hook! Yet I decided to apply this directive from Philippians 2:4: "Let each of you esteem *and* look upon *and* be concerned for not [merely] his own interests, but also each for the interests of others" (AMPLIFIED). If this was how Willard got his kicks, I decided I'd find something good about it, too.

The truth is that the only thing I liked about fishing was the company. But that was enough to make it enjoyable, both for me and for Willard. As I look back, what I would give to be able to go fishing with Willard again. Why is it that we often need to lose something in order to see its value?

The consequence of not working at mutual interests is too costly. When you make up your mind that your shared interests are few and you might as well go your separate ways, you've come to a fork in the road. From then on, you will grow further apart as friends. Eventually, you'll end up with a huge wall between you. Like too many people today, you may hear yourself complaining to your pastor or to a marriage counselor, "We just don't have anything in common anymore."

Giving yourself unselfishly to him and his interests will reverse this destructive tendency to pull apart. Our God is inventive, and you can ask Him for ideas to help you bridge the chasm of silence between you and your husband. God will help you take interest in your husband's work, hobbies, and habits. He will help you study your husband and know what makes him angry, amused, bored, happy, discouraged, or pleased. And the more you know him, the more your interest will thrill him.

Dealing with Disappointments

At the same time, I know that many women wish their husbands would pay attention to their interests. This, too, is important to building your friendship, since a good relationship is never one-sided. But I must offer a word of caution: Too often, we have high expectations, and when they aren't met, our hopes can be dashed. Then our relationship suffers badly, because we go about in stony silence, or else we pout. The cure for the sulks is to be flexible.

It took many big disappointments (and many days of tearful pouting, I'm embarrassed to say) for me to learn this basic lesson of flexibility. I was a great planner and loved to work out the details of a date with Willard long in advance. Eventually, our plans together became less and less frequent. Willard would also spring things on me, such as an evening out now and then. I found out I did not enjoy this last minute planning. I was growing frustrated. Finally, I brought up the issue with him. I didn't like what I discovered.

To my surprise, I found that he preferred to plan our dates together. But he had stopped making plans with me, because too often something came up to intervene, and then I would be terribly disappointed. As I said, I'd pout. So he learned not to promise anything, and that way he didn't have to deal with my disappointment. The alternative was to plan things on the spur of the moment, when he knew they would work out, even if neither of us liked it that way. And all because of my reaction!

One time, for example, we had planned a much-needed vacation after the fall harvest. We were going to go to Australia. We figured we needed three weeks to do the trip right. But as the time neared, we both came to the conclusion that we couldn't afford to be away from our business for that long just then. I knew that canceling our plans was the right decision, but I still found it hard to accept and didn't hide my disappointment.

At the root of my pouting was selfishness. When I looked beyond my own feelings, I realized Willard had been disappointed, too. I'd been too wrapped up in my own emotions to notice.

I also had to learn flexibility in our communication. Clear communication is another foundation stone of friendship. Unfortunately, husbands and wives don't always express their hopes and needs clearly.

As I've mentioned several times, Willard was a man of few words. When he spoke, his words were genuine and often full of wisdom. On the other hand, I have always been full of words—brimming over! This created stress in our marriage. You see, like so many women, I needed to hear those special words, "I love you." And I wanted to hear them often. But I didn't, so I wound up being hurt.

Once, when I told Willard about my hurt, he said, "If I tell you I love you as often as I know you want me to, I'm afraid the words will lose their meaning. I want it to be worth something when I say, 'I love you.'" I agreed with him, but it didn't take away my need to hear those words. So we worked out a little plan. When I needed to know he loved me, I would ask, "Do you?" and he would smile and simply say, "Yeah." That may sound a little silly, but it worked for us.

Staying Transparent

Another stone in the foundation of friendship is transparency—that is, the willingness to be open with each other about your innermost feelings and responses.

A popular saying not long ago was, "Love means never having to say you're sorry."[3] No way! Love means saying you're sorry over and over and over if necessary. And it means being able to bring up the things that hurt you.

Many Christians have the mistaken idea that they should never tell their mates—or anyone else—about things that hurt them. Somehow we think it's wrong to be offended, or we're too proud to admit we're still human and our feelings get bruised. Maybe we've grown up believing it's important to have "peace at any price." So we hide our feelings away—at least we think we're hiding them.

Something happens, however, when we try to conceal our emotions. Even if we think we've forgotten the offenses, they keep storing up inside of us. And then a small incident rubs us the wrong way, and it touches off an emotional explosion. The other person is left staring at us and wondering if we've gone off the deep end!

For others, this kind of explosion may never occur. We may be good at holding our tongues when we'd like to express our anger or bitterness. The problem is, we may hold our tongues but we still express hostility by the way we act. Buried anger can lead to depression, both physical and emotional coldness toward our husbands, or actions that are subtly aimed at hurting them.

The Bible gives the best solution for handling these emotions. "Do not let the sun go down while you are still angry" (Eph. 4:26 NIV). Some have called this "keeping short accounts." The principle is to deal with hurts as soon as possible, before they bury themselves in your spirit and become depression, bitterness, or rage. Don't let bitterness destroy your friendship with your spouse. Take the initiative to seek forgiveness or to build bridges where the relationship has been damaged.

Forgiveness

Let's look at forgiveness. Forgiveness is such an important part of friendship.

Basically, there is one tough and difficult step in restoring broken relationships—forgiveness. You must initiate, regardless of who is at fault, the extension of forgiveness. Go the second mile, the third mile. See your mate for the value you know is in your relationship. Forgiveness is when you release who has hurt you. You decide not to hurt him back. Yes, that means a willingness to swallow pride and hurt, to put your trust and emotions back out in the open where they run the risk of being hurt again.

Forgiveness is when the person becomes more important then the problem.

When we have been hurt, we all know we must forgive. But it is the forgetting that is so hard, especially when we have been deeply hurt by our mate. We must allow the oil of forgiveness to flow over the wound, and after forgiving over and over, that oil will heal the wound and it will not hurt so much.

Forgiveness is a wonderful gift we can give our mates. We must always keep in mind that we must forgive in order to be forgiven. Don't wait for your mate to repent. Waiting for our mate to repent before we forgive is to surrender our future to our mate. The first person to benefit from forgiving is the one who does it. What a sweet bond true forgiveness can give us, as we love each other for life.

I learned an important lesson in this regard from a dear friend named Linda, whom I came to know and love through the Good Shepherd and Families ministry. One time Linda did something that caused me to take offense. When she found I was offended, she came to me and said, "I didn't mean that the way you took it." The next thing she said changed the way I've viewed friendships ever since. She said, "Don't you know that I love you too much to hurt you intentionally? Please remember that the next time I do something that offends you."

Sooner or later, every friend will do something that offends or hurts us, especially the friend who lives the closest to us. Perhaps more than learning how to express our hurts, we need to take less notice of them. We need to tolerate errors, to see them as the result of human frailty, and show the same kind of forgiving grace God shows when He covers our sins. Hebrews 12:15 says, "See to it that no one misses the grace of God and that no bitter root grows up to cause trouble and defile many" (NIV). The best antidote for bitterness is the kind of grace I've been describing.

As we cultivate this attitude of grace, it will become easier to be transparent about our positive feelings. Affirming your husband will build that strongly founded friendship you desire. When you affirm each other with true sincerity, you will build a bond of friendship such as you never thought possible. Words are tools: Use them to build, not to tear down. Affirm, and your friendship will grow.

When it comes to transparency, one often overlooked area is being open in your appreciation of your husband's character and what he does for you. Too often, a woman fails to express her appreciation, which is to her detriment.

An extreme case, perhaps, is that of a woman I know. She's something of a perfectionist, and early in her marriage when her husband would buy her gifts, she always found that they weren't "quite right." Perhaps the color was a shade off, or perhaps it wasn't just the right, up-to-the minute design. There was inevitably some reason to take the gift back and exchange it for something of her own choosing. Eventually her husband gave up. When she spoke to me about her situation, she mournfully wished she had never criticized but had expressed appreciation—for now she has to buy and even wrap her own Christmas presents if she wants something under the tree! Her husband refuses to shop for her at all.

When you express appreciation for a man and what he does for you, it's more than likely you'll see one important result: He will love to do good things for you. Nothing brings about good results like reward.

Singing His Praises

One more foundation stone on which your friendship with your husband can be built solid is honoring him before others. In Proverbs 31, the godly wife is portrayed as one whose husband is "known in the city gates" (v. 23). By this, Solomon meant that her husband is respected in the community, based on his wife's reports about him.

Think about this for a moment: Would your husband's friends, family, and brothers and sisters in Christ respect him because of your reports about him? Or do they mostly know his flaws and perhaps even hidden sins because of your "sharing"?

Every once in a while, when Willard was on a trip, he would run into someone who knew me but had not met him before. It was so gratifying to me when he would come home from one of those chance meetings, beaming from ear to ear, and say, "This person told me, 'From all that LeeAnn has said about you, I can hardly wait to get to know you. You must be a remarkable man.'"

To so many people, you are your husband's only representative. How do you represent him? I so much wanted to set my husband apart, to have people respect him for the man he was. This has two beautiful results. First, good reports have a way of getting back to the person you've complimented. Second, when you love and respect someone in this way, you can be sure he will speak lovingly of you.

After Willard's death, a friend who had gone with him on a fishing trip to Alaska called on me one day. He told me that one evening, as they were sitting around the campfire with their guide, Willard got up and went into the tent. The guide then turned to our friend and said, "That Willard sure is a quiet one. But one thing I know about him, he really loves his wife!"

I will probably never know on this side of eternity exactly what good things Willard said about me to that stranger. But I know that if I were in his position I would have been saying good things about him too. You see, you can't lose by loving.

Leading psychologists tell us there are two emotional needs inside every human being: to love and to be loved. Your relationship with your husband is one of the most important relationships in your entire span of years on this earth. Love him enough to make him your friend, your best friend. You will never be sorry you did.

We are never more fulfilled than when we make the one we choose as our mate feel loved. Love "bears all things, believes all things, hopes all things, endures all things" (1 Cor. 13:7 NKJV). What is fulfillment? It is to love and be loved. God puts in each of us a deep desire to love and be loved. True loving is thinking about others and their happiness first. To be accepting is something that can't be measured. To have the security of being truly loved is priceless. All the success in a career cannot give the joy and contentment that being loved by someone gives to us. There is nothing wrong with being successful; it's good and can strengthen your marriage. But success without love and acceptance is of no value. It's empty success. One way to attain this wonderful reward is to love. You can never love too much. Unselfish love can only bring love in return. Remember I said *unselfish* love... there is such a difference. What is unselfish love? Selfishness destroys us. Unselfishness builds us up. True love has unlimited endurance; it is able to endure all obstacles, and it even loves in the face of unreturned love. Galatians 5:3 tells us we should be free to serve each other in love. Sometimes there are cases where it takes years of loving, then loving and loving some more, but it does pay off.

Chapter Six

For the Sake of Your Children

Proverbs 31 talks about the "wife of noble character" who is "worth far more than rubies" (v. 1). Perhaps the most beautiful promise for any mother is found toward the end of this chapter: "Her children rise up and call her blessed" (v. 28 NKJV).

All Christian women would like to be known for the kind of noble character described in this passage. Yet so many of us struggle with poor self-image and the feeling that others don't respect or value us—especially our own children. Sadly, parents today often take the attitude that whether or not their children grow up to love and respect them, or whether they live in a godly way is just a matter of chance. This is not true.

There is something we can do to ensure that our children will call us blessed. We can live in a way that will make them say, "My mother is happy, blessed by God, and is a godly woman. I want the same kind of godly marriage she and Dad shared." What a blessing to think that we can have this kind of effect on our children! And the key to such an influence is to love the father of your children.

In my research on raising children, I read about some things that are important in raising godly children. There are no words that speak as loudly as our actions. Live out what you want your children to hear. We all have heard, "Your actions speak so loudly I cannot hear what you are saying." I do not think we realize what an impact our actions have on our children's lives. This is true for the negative as well as the positive.

Being an example is so important and so essential for the well being of your child. If you give them this foundation it will help see them through the rough places of life. Most problems between parents and children are really problems between parents.

In the lives of my sons, this security proved to be a strong factor in what they faced in losing their father at such a young age.

If you have been divorced from the father of your children, I'm not trying to put you off. Even a divorced woman can show respect for her former husband, by refusing to belittle him or recite all his faults in front of your children. Many women do this because they fear their former husbands may be talking them down to the children, and they want to win the children to their side. But there will be time enough when the children are grown to give them a more mature view of what went wrong. And you can do more to win your children—not just to yourself, but also to a godly viewpoint—by always speaking words of respect for your former spouse. This will impress your children far more than name-calling or complaining.

For those who are struggling with the everyday rough spots of marriage, the same rule applies: If you want to make a godly impact on your children, love their father! You see, in child rearing we need to keep two simple and basic principles in mind.

First, a father probably has the greatest influence on his children's self-image. Christian counselors have learned that an individual's childhood view of his earthly father usually becomes his view of his heavenly Father. If a mother teaches her child that Dad is to be respected, the child will grow to have an innate respect for God as well. If a mother plants rebellion, complaining, and mistrust in a child's heart, he is likely to struggle not only against his father, but against God, too. Obviously, this is not what we want for our children.

I painfully recall a Christian couple who had two lovely daughters. For reasons unknown to me, the father drifted away from God and his family. He began to drink, got involved with another woman, and spent less and less time with his girls. Consequently, they developed a deep sense of feeling rejected.

As they grew and their father became untrustworthy, the girls manifested those negative feelings in their behavior—especially the older daughter. She quit attending church and fell deeply into sin, searching for the male love that should have come from her dad. She also refused to trust or worship God, not realizing how her perception of Him had been tainted by her father's example.

Unfortunately, the last I heard of this young woman, she had shown up on a friend's doorstep. She was drunk and immodestly dressed, and she tearfully reported that she was planning to go live with her father who had moved to another state. I can't overstate how important a father is to his children's self-image and their perception of God.

Second, the childhood home is the primary training ground for marriage. Young people get their view of marriage, the roles they are to play in a later adult relationship and what their homes will be like, from the homes in which they grow up.

It's heartbreaking to think of the climbing divorce rate in America and other Western countries. By conservative estimates, fifty percent of marriages in the U.S. end in divorce.[1] And there is no way to tell how vast is the number of children who are growing up in what are known as "dysfunctional homes"—homes in which there are serious martial or emotional problems. All this heartache can do nothing but breed more pain and insecurity.

For the years Willard and I were in music ministry, we were repeatedly exposed to poor marriage relationships. In talking with those who came up for prayer or a word of counseling after we sang, we saw how their parents' bad marriages had hindered their job performance and their relationships with their spouses, children, and the Lord. This was most visible during the visits we made to correctional facilities. We sang one song in particular that assured our listeners they were loved and special. Time and again, those hardened men and women would come up to us weeping, confessing that no one had ever told them they were special. They would usually spill out a story about having grown up in a home where their parents hated each other or fought constantly.

It's plain, then, that the destruction brought by a loveless marriage is echoed through the generations. So let's focus on positive, life-building things we can do to affect our children for good.

Willard and I certainly didn't have a perfect marriage. But we loved each other very much. Because I had been brought up in a home where my mother loved and respected my father, I knew this was the right thing to do—even when I felt hurt, neglected, or did not agree with a certain decision. The benefit of those choices has spilled over into the lives of others in surprising ways.

For instance, one of our sons had a young friend who spent a lot of time in our home while growing up. This person wrote and told me things after Willard's death that still bring tears to my eyes:

> Watching you in everyday situations has caused my view of marriage to be restored. As you know, I came from a broken home where my parent's marriage ended in divorce. For a long time, I felt that I didn't really want to be married because of all the hurt and bitterness I saw in marriage.
>
> Being around you caused me to see what God really intended marriage to be all about. In fact, it was through you that I found the strength and confidence to be able to commit myself to marriage.
>
> Your wonderful relationship was a miracle in my life, because Jesus used your love for each other as an example of a healthy, happy, loving Christian marriage. I will be forever grateful for the healing effect the two of you together have had on my life.

Never underestimate the effects of a godly, loving marriage. How can you love your husband in such a way as to sow seeds of godliness, peace, and joy in the lives of your children?

Support Their Father's Authority

The first thing I recommend is to have a loving respect for your husband and his place of authority in the home. Your respect will be an example to your children, helping them to grow up with respect for authority and for God's laws and His Word. This will make it easier for them to understand leadership and what it means to be a leader when their time comes to go into the world on their own. It's vital to remember that a man is no more of a leader than he is with his own children. Women either contribute to a respect for their leadership or undermine them.

One of the most common ways women undermine their husband's authority is in the process of disciplining the children. A man has the God-given responsibility for the discipline and order of his household. He should set the disciplinary standards for the children. Because men are generally tough-minded when it comes to discipline and women tend to be gentler, conferring brings a good balance. But as in all other areas, the man is to have the final authority.

The problem comes when you take sides with your children against a decision their dad has made. This often happens because you think a punishment is too strict or given out too quickly, without knowledge of all the circumstances, or simply because your husband was tired and irritable. These things may be true, but you should never take sides with your children against their father. Children can easily read our attitudes.

The problem can be compounded when your husband becomes aware that you're siding with the children and he feels you're being disloyal to him. He may also feel that you're trying to win the children to yourself.

Willard and I learned a lot about this by observing other couples, even before we had our children. Often we would see a father correct his child, only to have his wife openly or in a subtle way disagree with his correction. Sometimes we saw women be strongly critical of their husband's correction. This is confusing to a child. It says to him, "Your father is cruel and unjust. I love you more than he does." And when a woman lets her children think they can come to her if they don't agree with Dad's direction or authority, it can breed in them a deceitful and manipulative spirit. Men know exactly what's going on when women do this. It's little wonder they get angry!

I can't say I always agreed with Willard's correction of our sons. But three things helped me in this: First, I knew of his deep love for the boys, even though I sometimes thought he was too strict. Second, he was consistent. He didn't punish them in fits of anger, and when he promised a punishment, they got it. Third, when the boys were spanked—sometimes, I felt, too hard—it always amazed and blessed me to see them crawl up on his lap for comfort when it was all over.

But when there was unfair discipline or spanking that I thought was too hard, I kept one rule in mind—when I confronted or appealed to Willard, it was in private. I never wanted to cause a split between Willard and the children or to undermine his authority over them. And because he knew I was protecting his position of authority, he was much more willing to consider my opinion.

The underlying principle is this: God intends child rearing to bring a husband and wife together in learning how to work with each other. Too often, parents let issues of child discipline pull them apart. But if you learn to work together, you and your children will be much better off.

Love Their Father Best

A second major way you can sow good seeds in the lives of your children is to place your love for your husband before your love for them. This sounds contradictory, but it's not.

This is another area in which relationships between husbands and wives break down. As soon as the first child comes along, many women feel torn, or they set their first love for their husband aside. They think, after all, this baby is so tiny and helpless, and my husband is a grown man. He doesn't need me as much as our child. It's true that we go through seasons when the welfare of our small children, especially infants, takes a major effort. And neither do we have to neglect our children in order to place our love for our husbands in first place. I'm advocating a balance, of course.

Now that my sons are grown and have children of their own, it is so rewarding for me to watch as they raise their little ones and to see them follow much in their father's footsteps. I notice improvement in areas where we missed the boat. What a joy it is to me, a grandmother now, to see my sons doing such a good job with those wonderful grandchildren I love so much. It makes me smile when I think how, even now when a grandchild needs to be disciplined or spanked, my heart still says, please no, while my head says, yes this is good. I am so grateful my sons had a good example of a wonderful father.

It was hard for me to place my love for the children in proper perspective. Whenever Willard wanted to do something special just with me, I'd say, "We can take the children, too, can't we?" It was so hard for me to leave them when they were younger. Eventually, in response to my neglect of him in favor of the boys, Willard got in the habit of turning on the TV and falling asleep after dinner. I became defensive and spent even more time fussing with our sons.

It took an eye-opening experience—finding worn-out sheets in the linen closet, chipped china, and a dented table-top—to make me realize our marriage had lost its sparkle. And it took letting go of my motherly over-protectiveness of my sons to begin rebuilding our marriage relationship.

Demonstrating that you love and cherish your mate means spending time together. Taking time for each other is one thing many couples do not do, especially after they've been together for awhile. When you take time to be together, you find that you automatically share dreams and hopes. A relationship works much easier when you're not trying to read each other's mind. When children are around, however, time alone together is difficult to find.

I recall the days when it seemed we couldn't carry on an adult conversation because every other sentence was interrupted. Usually the interruption was a matter of life and death, of course. ("I can't find my Superman shirt!" or "My baseball glove isn't on top of the car where I left it!") The carefree days of young marriage were gone, but Willard and I determined that the romance didn't have to disappear.

After our get-away weekend to San Francisco, we decided we were going to demonstrate our oneness to the children. For example, it was just a small thing, but we decided we would no longer allow the children to sit between us. (It's amazing how often a small child will wiggle his way in between adults!) They could sit beside us, or sometimes on our laps, but never between us.

Because it was so hard to get time to talk alone, Willard and I had a hot tub built into our new home. We loved to bathe together, and we also found it to be about the only waking hour when we could talk without interruption. The bathroom door was locked, and unless there was a dire emergency, the boys knew they were not to bother us.

Now I'm not suggesting you have to take on our rules for your household, though you may want to. But if I get across nothing else in this book, I will stress this: Communicate with your man. Be creative. Make your solutions to problems fun. Keep refining your marriage and your home life until you find the things that work best for you.

Nevertheless, the basic principle holds: Put your love for your husband first. Don't allow your children to come between you and him in matters of discipline, affection, or communication.

The Result: Secure Children

After Willard died, each of my sons told me the same thing in his own way. "One of the best things Dad left us was the blessing of knowing that he loved you, Mom." And now that they're more mature, they can see that of all the good things Willard did with them—hunting, fishing, sports—the most important thing he did for them was to give them security through our stable, loving relationship. I know this inner security gave the boys great strength when they went through the trauma of losing their father. They were a true support to me because they were secure in themselves.

Proverbs 31:28 says to me that it is well-adjusted, healthy, secure children who can give themselves to others. Children whose parents have bad marriages generally don't like to stick around the home. But when you have a good marriage, your love will be attractive, and it will draw your children back to your side, where they will bless you. And what a blessing that is!

Loving your husband is the first step to creating a home that is a spiritual and emotional shelter for the hearts of your children. You can create a home where your children not only grow into the godly children you want them to be, but also into godly parents. It is such a blessing to watch your child being a good parent. Then as the years roll on, what an added blessing it is to see their children raising their children in godly ways. Create a home out of your house for your children and husband. A happy Christian home is centered on people, not things. It is a place where there is flexibility and where the welfare of all is considered.

Chapter Seven

Loving Your Husband for a Dark Tomorrow

It seems we often see things best only in contrast. Darkness makes light seem lighter and death makes life seem brighter. Loss makes us appreciate so much more the love we have today, flaws and all.

We are not promised any tomorrows, nor are we promised that all our tomorrows will be bright. And when my dark tomorrow came, I prayed, "Does it have to be so dark, Lord?"

The first thing I did after Willard's death was to look back at all our beautiful memories. I remembered the love we shared as young newlyweds, the joy of bringing home our first tender-skinned newborn, the struggles and joys of building up our farming business, the years of sitting side-by-side with Willard in church. Pictures of the past flooded into my head.

These wonderful memories made me realize how important it is to live each day with someone as if it were our last. As never before, I saw the need to not let the sun go down while we are still angry (Eph. 4:26) and to live without regrets. In the days right after Willard's death, however, one thought kept crossing my mind—how long could I live on memories?

Later, we'll look at some of the spiritual lessons you'll need to know to go on with your life when you have lost a loved one by death, divorce, or separation, or even if you're a married woman forced to fend for yourself. But here I want to discuss some very practical things you need to know now in the event of a dark tomorrow.

Financial Matters

Some men feel they are doing their wives a favor by not involving them in financial, business, or insurance matters. Many women feel this is a favor, too. In fact, some Christian women wrongly consider this as being sheltered from the world by their husbands, who are their "spiritual covering." A husband is to be his wife's covering. But that means he is the one responsible in the final analysis of the family's spiritual, physical, emotional, and financial well-being. He must set the tone and direction in these areas, but God did not mean for your husband to bear these burdens alone.

In Genesis 2:18, we read that God created Eve to be "a helper suitable for him." That means you are to be a helper who is fitted to your husband and capable of assisting him in all areas of life. To do that, we must be informed and involved in all his affairs insofar as it is possible.

Choosing to be involved has a lot of pluses as well as minuses. It takes much understanding and patience on the part of both husband and wife. You may have days when you ask, "Is it really worth it?" The answer is yes. For one thing, you will find great need to work at your communication, and whenever you do that, your love grows. You'll also have a greater understanding of the pressures on your husband. And, of course, it will make you better able to handle your business and financial matters alone in the event that it becomes necessary.

God's ways are always best. He wants us to put each other first. Several years after Willard's death, I realized how true this was. When Willard and I went to San Francisco for that weekend, we decided to change some things in our marriage. He would spend more time with the boys and not so much time becoming a successful businessman. I would spend more time being involved with our businesses and not so much time with the boys. As I said earlier, he, wanting to be successful, and I, wanting to be the best mom, was not wrong. We had just got them out of proportion. So we made the decision that weekend to change it.

God is so good and honored our desires to do what we needed to do. Because Willard decided to spend more time with our boys, they have so many more memories of the wonderful times they had with their dad. Memories they may not have had, had he not made that decision. Then, because I decided to be more involved with the businesses, I was much more capable of taking over when Willard died. We never know what the fringe benefits will be when we listen to the Lord. So learn from your mistakes and right decisions. Do what it takes to put each other first.

I am aware that sometimes the business is such that you cannot or do not desire to be that involved. But be interested in what your man does and have a plan of what would happen if you were left responsible.

Shortly after Willard's death, I came across a special section in *Farm Wife News* on the subject of going on alone. It offered the following list of materials and information a woman should gather to prepare for the possibility of being on her own:

1. **Life insurance.** Where are the policies kept? List your policies by company, policy number, face amount, agent, pre-
   mium due date, and any loans against the policy.

2. **Safe-deposit box.** What is the number and location? Where
   are the keys kept?

3. **Mortgages, leases, and other periodic payments.** When
   are they due? List the amounts, names, and addresses of
   those to whom these are payable and the repayment terms.

4. **Real estate holdings.** Where are the deeds or contracts
   kept? Itemize each, with the approximate value, price paid,
   any mortgage, and the names of joint owners, if any.

5. **Other items.** Bank accounts; titles of vehicles; installment
   payments (due dates and amounts); moneys owed to family
   and others; Social Security cards; old income tax returns and
   cancelled checks; account books or other business books;
   partnerships and other business agreements; stocks, futures
   or forward contracts held and the name of the broker; burial
   plots and arrangements; preferred guardian for your children;
   executor or trustee preferred; name and address of your
   lawyer; name and address of your accountant.[1]

This list can be tailored to your individual situation and
needs. Once all the materials are gathered, make several copies
of everything. Put one in a safe deposit box or other secure
place. This could save hours of searching and worry at a time
when you don't need the added pressure of wondering if your
affairs are in order.

One more thing that is so important in keeping your affairs
in order is to have a will. A will is relatively simple to do. But it
seems so easy to put off—especially easy for young couples. You
may think you do not have anything to leave that is of any

importance. But remember that if you have children, they are the most precious gift of all you are leaving. I was so grateful Willard and I had this in order. When we were younger, some of our young friends were both killed in a car accident. They left a small child and they did not have a will. Because of this, there was much strife between their families. Who should this young child go to? It is so easy to think when we are young that this will not happen to us. I am sure that was the thinking of this young couple. Don't let the future of the most precious commodity you have on earth be left in the hands of the state.

Funeral Arrangements

People often have a hard time discussing their spouse's wishes in the event of death. Christians can take the attitude, "I don't want to think about death, because I've got the life of Christ in me. My spirit is going on to live with Jesus, so what do I care what they do with my physical body?" I don't mean to be disrespectful about such a private subject, but when you die, somebody will be left to do something with your body! It is an act of love and wisdom to discuss these matters in advance.

This is an area none of us likes to think about. But when you lose your mate, it is all very real. Many decisions need to be made. As I think back on those awful days, I wish that we had done even more to make this time easier for me. As I said earlier, you think you are too young and these kinds of decisions just don't have to be made yet. I knew that Willard had often said he did not think viewing the body was necessary, because that person was not there any more. But I found that when someone goes so quickly, you really do need to get it in your head that they really are gone, and going to the mortuary did help us. When my sons and I went to view the body, when I looked on his face, he seemed so at peace. And I felt the Lord wrap His arms around me and say to me in my heart, "See, he is with Me." My brother who was there with us said, "Sis, what happened? Your countenance just changed." So I relayed what I had just felt.

One never knows what God will use to bring just the comfort you need when you need it. We did have a burial plot, so that was already decided. But if you can bring yourself to it, sit down and tell each other what you would like. It would make all those decisions you need to make so much easier on the one who is left.

Another great idea I heard was that each year at the beginning of the year a husband should sit down and write a letter to his wife. In this letter he should list all the different insurance you pay, to whom, when, etc. Also, list the investments you have, where they are held, and all the details about them. List any debts you might have, or who is a debtor to you, their payment schedule, etc. He should include in this letter all the things that would make it easier for his wife if something should happen to him. Then tell her how much you love her. Put this letter in a safe place. A place you both know about such as a safe-deposit box.

It would be a blessing to your man to write him a letter also each year. In this letter tell him how to operate the washing machine and how to sort clothes and about spotting the stains. And tell him where all the music lessons are given, or any other place you take the kids. Maybe you could even copy some of his or the children's most favorite recipes. List whatever you can think of to make things easier for him. Make some meal plans for a couple of weeks. It might be helpful for you to list the birthdays of the kids. Of course, always close your letter with how much you love him. Then find that special place to keep it.

Try to think of how hard this time will be for your mate and put anything in these letters that would help each other through this hard time and make their job just a little easier. Things change so fast, so be sure and update your letter each year.

If you love your husband, you will become his "suitable helper" today. He will then have the comfort of knowing you will be able to function well in the event of a dark tomorrow.

Separation

Even if you don't lose your spouse to a premature death, I am well aware that many women face another kind of dark tomorrow. They can suffer the same kind of grief when their marriages break up. Unfortunately, Christian couples are not exempt from these pressures.

When problems arise in a marriage, too many Christian women these days are tempted to think, "Why not just get a divorce? After all, we're under grace, aren't we?" If you're in a difficult position and are thinking these thoughts, first I want to encourage you: Divorce is not the answer that non-Christians and the media make it out to be. I don't feel capable of addressing the theological issues surrounding divorce. Besides, others have already done so. But I do want you to consider some of the far-reaching, emotional ramifications of divorce.

I remember so well the first summer after Willard's death when Rob, our youngest son, who had just turned fifteen, went to basketball camp. While he was there I received a letter from him. He wrote, "Mom, we have gone though an awful time these past few months. I miss Dad so much. But you know what? There is a boy in my room here at camp, and his mom and dad are getting a divorce. It really is a lot worse. He has to make a choice who he will live with. At least I didn't have to choose."

Divorce is so hard on our children. Think hard before you make that choice. I must say that God is in the redeeming business, and if you find yourself in a divorce, ask Him to come alongside your children and give them grace.

Right after Willard's death (and probably because I was going through my grieving process), I became especially aware of people who were separated or divorced. I could sense in them the same kind of deep loneliness I was experiencing. And there was another feeling, too. They were struggling with the sense of rejection. They had been rejected by their spouses, so they were pulling away into a shell, isolating themselves from their friends and their brothers and sisters in Christ.

For those of you who have friends who are experiencing a dark tomorrow, don't allow them to pull away from you. I know we often just don't know what to say to help them, so we don't say anything. We even tend to leave them alone. Anything is better than nothing. Reach out to those who are going through a dark time. Reach out in love and understanding. A good thing to remember is that often after six months or so, everyone tends to forget. It is then that your friends who have gone though a dark tomorrow really need you to be there for them.

You cannot allow grief, whether because of death or divorce, to separate you from those who can give you love and support. True, times of quiet and being alone are necessary to work through grief. But more than that, you need the affirmation of friends. You need to be exposed to the common, ongoing aspects of life, for life does go on whether you want it to at the moment or not!

God so opened the windows of heaven to me and poured down His love on me. In that first year, I received over 2,500 cards and letters. You really do need each other in your dark times. Sometimes it is hard to see that, but it is so true. So don't miss those times to reach out and touch a friend, even if it seems small and insignificant to you.

This makes me think of something very special a friend did for me during this time. When my second son, Lonnie, got married that next year, she came to me and said, "I want to lend my husband to be with you during the wedding. Get him a tux and let him stand in for Willard." At first I thought, No, I cannot do this, but later I decided it would be so helpful. After all, her husband was one of Willard's very best friends, so why not? It truly was a blessing for us that day. God knows what you need. Let Him supply those needs.

Second, for those who want a divorce, consider that divorce is not the end of a relationship, especially when there are children involved. When a married couple with children decide to divorce, they never lose their connection because of their children. At the time of the divorce, the wife may think, "Well, we'll file for joint custody—I'll have them during the week, and he can see them every other weekend." But the decisions and struggles of child rearing don't end here. It's not as simple as a one-time decision. Raising children requires many decisions and lots of dialogue concerning holidays, vacations, and so on. If your inability to communicate or love your husband is a major obstacle, how much more struggle will you have when you need to communicate about delicate and important issues that involve your children?

Some dear friends of ours saw their marriage end in divorce. Afterward, the usual discussions about such things, as where their sons would spend Christmas, were complicated by the fact that the father had moved to another state. Later, when the boys reached high school age, they said they wanted to live with Dad rather than Mom, because he was more permissive. Naturally, a whole new round of talks followed. And when the sons were ready to marry, their divided loyalties created the need for still another level of diplomacy.

Truly, children tie a father and mother together for life. Knowing the open attitude about divorce today, I write these things with real caution. I also pray that God's wisdom and love will come through my words, because the last thing I want to do is point the finger at someone who is in a difficult marriage or who has already gone through divorce. I believe divorce is a sin, but it's a sin like any other and can be dealt with by turning your heart to God.

For those of you going through a dark tomorrow today, I want to affirm one more time that *you just cannot lose by loving.* Even in a situation that ends in a way you don't want, or when it seems your prayers aren't answered, you are not the loser if you love until the end.

To all wives, I want to say: Love with all your heart today. Then no matter what tomorrow brings, whether joy and oneness or the sorrow of separation, you will have lived a rich life, and its inner rewards will go on and on.

Chapter Eight

Going On

Like the previous chapter, this one is written to women who have lost their husbands. Your loss may have come through death or divorce. Or perhaps you have lost your husband emotionally. It may seem, like the prodigal son, he is in a far country and you're waiting, hoping he will come home to your heart.

At once, you may be saying, "I don't want to go on living without a loving husband at my side. I don't think I'm strong enough to do it." I can honestly say I know exactly how you feel. When Willard went to be with the Lord, my wonderful world fell apart. Not long thereafter, a friend came to tell me that other friends were asking, "What is poor LeeAnn going to do now without Willard?"

"What did you tell them?" I asked.

"I told them you're tough," my friend said, smiling. "I told them you'll make it."

The truth was that I didn't feel tough at all. Many days, I sat on the sofa, feeling devastated, not knowing which way to turn or what to do next. I didn't want to go on. This may be hard for some to understand, but I was brokenhearted and didn't even want to go on living. Being on my own made me feel unfulfilled and empty. What's more, there seemed to be no one to whom I could reveal my true feelings.

Keeping a Journal

So I began to do something that helped me get a handle on all the rampaging emotions I felt. It's something simple that any woman can do in order to begin ministering to herself in hard times—keep a journal.

Right after Willard's death, friends kept coming to tell me what Willard had meant to them. Some told how much our love for each other and our solid marriage had meant to them. I can remember thinking, through the numbness, "I'll have to write all these good things down so I can recall them later. Maybe it will be helpful for the boys." A close friend prompted me to write these stories down as well. She seemed to feel urgency about capturing on paper the things I had learned about the love of a woman for her husband. Somewhere inside of me I felt this prompting, too. But to be honest, I did nothing about it at first.

Eventually, another close friend heard about my desire to have a record of my years with Willard, and she gave me a little blank book in which to write about them. The first friend I mentioned had done some writing down of the stories for me, so I transferred these things into my own little book. I recorded events that were funny and touching and many that were very personal. I called this book my "Bear It Book," because when I was hurting, I could open it up. Just rereading my entries became a source of strength.

One of my heartwarming entries concerned a little neighbor boy named Reed. He loved Willard so much and enjoyed teasing him. Reed's mom told me that a night or two after Willard's death, as she was tucking him in bed, Reed asked, "What do you think is going on in heaven? Do you think there are tractors there?" She thought for a moment, then replied, "Well, Reed, heaven is a happy place, so if you want a tractor there, there will probably be tractors."

Reed asked, "What kind of tractors do you think they have there?"

"I suppose they have whatever kind you want—Ford, John Deere, or whatever."

"I guess that takes care of that." Reed said. "Willard's driving a Ford."

The next night at bedtime, Reed asked, "Mom, what do you think is going on in heaven tonight? Do you suppose they have tractor pulls?"

His mother smiled, now knowing what her five-year-old was thinking. He had seen Willard participate in a tractor pull shortly before his death, and Willard's Ford had out-pulled his dad's John Deere. She remembered all the fun Willard had shared with Reed after that victory, showing him the trophy and joking about the contest. So she said, "I suppose they just might have tractor pulls if that's what you want."

"Brother," Reed said, "that means I'm going to have to look at all those dumb trophies Willard wins when I get there."

After recording this story in my journal, I wrote, "Jesus is so good. He knew I needed to hear this sweet child's thoughts. Even the children loved Willard. Who didn't?"

Dwelling on the good things life has given us makes the dark, discouraging days so much more bearable. As the apostle

Paul said, "Whatever is true...noble...right...pure... lovely... admirable—if anything is excellent or praiseworthy—think about such things" (Phil. 4:8 NIV).

My "Bear It Book" was truly a joy. But some months after I began it, yet another friend came to me and said, "LeeAnn, your book is such a good idea, and I know it's very helpful for you. But don't you have any bad feelings, too? You can't just keep them all bottled up inside. So what are you going to do with them?" I admitted to her that there were many feelings I'd been suppressing—thoughts like, Why am I alone now? And prayers like, "God, why weren't you there to save Willard's life when I needed you?"

You may laugh, but a short time later, another friend went out and bought me another little blank book! This one I called my "Ugly Book." On its pages, I recorded all the bad feelings I was experiencing. I kept track of the questioning prayers I prayed, as well as the Scripture verses (1 Thess 4:13-18; Ps. 56:8; Heb. 13:5) and other answers that came into my head in response to those "why" kind of prayers.

My "Ugly Book" also became a source of strength. First, it gave me an outlet for my feelings when I was too upset to let them show to other people. Second, it gave me a record to look at when I heard myself praying those "why" prayers again and again. Then I could see God's replies to my questions and feel His comfort all over again.

One of the principles I learned from this simple act of keeping a journal was that when God prompts you to do something, go ahead and do it. I found that obeying these small promptings opened the way to greater things I could not have imagined.

Opening Up

Writing became one source of comfort for me, a way of ministering to my own soul. But there was a second kind of ministry

I had to become open to—the ministry from others. This was more difficult than I could have imagined.

I've already mentioned the friends who were around me. Yet I felt a great distance from them at first because I hurt so much inside, and like a wounded animal, I didn't want anyone to get close enough to touch the pain. Many of us also have an inbred kind of pride, and it comes as an inner voice that says, "Come on. Be strong. This is what everyone expects from you. You can't ask people to put up with your tears. Put on a smile, and be brave."

The apostle Paul wrote, however, "Bear one another's burdens, and in this way you will fulfill the law of Christ" (Gal. 6:2 NRSV). How can others minister to us if we are prideful and unwilling to open up and reveal our feelings?

Eventually, I found that I had to let others inside to see the real me—the me who wasn't strong, who didn't have all the Christian answers ready at hand, who sometimes got mad at God, and did not understand in the least why my husband had died. It was in allowing others to handle this pain with me that much more healing came.

I recall how one friend phoned me from a city halfway across the country; "LeeAnn," she said, "I am calling to say that I don't know what to say." How her honesty and vulnerability touched me. Other friends affected me in similar ways. Cards, phone calls, visits—all these small acts of caring added up to a shower of love. When others reached out to me, it became easier to share the lonely times. When the hurt was more than I could bear any longer, it seemed that someone would phone or drop by. I came to see these "coincidences" as God's way of nudging the people who helped me bear my burden.

Trusting God

The apostle Paul encouraged us, saying, "Cast all your anxiety on him because he cares for you" (1 Pet. 5:7 NIV). It isn't so hard, really, to cast your cares upon the Lord. What's hard is leaving them there! So often we feel that God is not working fast enough to heal our hurts or to answer our prayers. We become impatient. It is so hard to relax in Him and trust Him, isn't it?

When all is going well, it's easy to say, "Of course I trust God," or "If you've got a problem, just trust God and He'll help you." These things come off the tongue so readily when we can see the road ahead. But the moment the wind of change is thrown at us and we're wandering blindly, there goes our trust. It need not be that way, however. In fact, when we're willing to launch out into God's care during these dark times, He is able to do something new and altogether wonderful with our lives.

Sometimes I like to try to turn the picture around by imagining what God feels like when we're slow to trust or refuse to hear and obey Him. Imagine the sadness from His point of view! Like a loving Father, He wants to fulfill our deepest needs—if only we will let go of our fear and take His hand. Then He'll lead us.

The most important ministry you need to help you recover from the devastation of loss, is the ministry God Himself wants to perform in your life. After all, He is the one best able to reach into the deepest places of your soul and bring the healing touch, isn't He?

In some ways, after Willard's death, I had to learn about trusting God all over again. I'd said for a long time that I trusted God, but that was when I had a husband to provide for me and give me love. Now that I had this terrifying sense of being alone on my own again, I wondered about God: Does He really know my needs? Can I trust Him to do the best thing for my life? My mind could say yes, but my heart was hesitant to answer.

As I think about trusting Him, I reflect back on a story. Once Willard and I visited Mexico. It was a bright, sunshiny day. After getting up early, I went down by the water to have my quiet-time and then enjoy breakfast at the restaurant in the hotel where we were staying. Willard was not a breakfast man, so he stayed in bed longer that morning. I was sitting there eating my food and thinking, *What a nice looking Mexican family just came in*. They approached me and ask if I minded if they shared my table. I learned they were from Guadalajara and were visiting there in Puerto Vallarta. He saw my Bible beside me and started asking questions about my walk with Jesus. Hard questions I really did not have answers for. I felt Jesus tell me to answer that I just simply needed to "trust Him."

Before long, Willard joined us for his usual cup of coffee. He too joined in on our conversation. We shared a long time that morning with our new friends. Over the years we corresponded often with them. One of the things he often mentioned in his letters was how it stood out in his mind that we'd said, "You just have to trust Him." As I look back on that, I feel it was so easy to share that with him then when everything was going so wonderfully well in our lives, but now that all had fallen apart for me, just trusting Him seemed so hard. BUT—just trusting Him is the only way we *can* go on, and there is such peace and rest in complete trust in Him.

God's Ways are Not Our Ways

A number of friends had suggested I develop my "Bear It Book" into a larger manuscript that might be helpful to other women. As one friend put it, in Titus 2:3 the Bible says that the older women are to teach the younger women how to love their husbands. That made me one of the older women! I didn't think I was ready for that. Besides...write a book? I've never even been good at spelling. I pushed the idea out of my mind.

In the meantime, my son Mark and his wife, Laurie, decided to become involved with an international organization called

Youth With a Mission (YWAM). We'd known about this excellent ministry for some time and were happy with the work they were doing in training and sending missionaries to nations all around the world. I thought it was a good idea for Mark and Laurie to try a short-term venture through YWAM. And after they became involved, I decided to take part in a special YWAM school for people in their middle years. This school, appropriately known as Crossroads Discipleship Training Course, altered my life.

During one of the morning sessions, a man from California named Dan Sneed was talking to us about learning to hear God's voice. (Knowing you can hear God's voice is, of course, a necessary step in learning to trust Him.) I had heard that this man was blessed with a special gift of insight from God.

You must understand that I'm the conservative type. I believe that when God speaks to you through another person, it will be to confirm something He has already communicated to you in your heart. So I felt quite reserved when, at the end of the session, Dan Sneed said he was going to demonstrate how God could communicate to us through special gifts He gives to others in the body of Christ. Though feeling reserved, I couldn't escape the feeling I'd had on my way to school that God was going to give me some special direction for my life here.

The session was to end at noon, and of the eighty-seven people in the class, Dan had spoken to many, but not to me. Was I relieved or disappointed? I couldn't tell. But just when I thought he was going to end the session, Dan looked at me. He pointed me out and asked my name.

"LeeAnn," he said, "you sing, don't you?" Though I was speechless, my roommate quickly confirmed it. "In fact," Dan went on, "the Lord has confirmed to me that you were involved in a singing ministry for a long time—a family group."

My mind raced, thinking about our eighteen years with the Good Shepherd Quartet and Families. How could this stranger know these things unless the Lord was revealing them to him? He certainly had my attention.

"This group was your identity, but you were not completely fulfilled in it."

"Please, God," I prayed silently, "don't tell him *everything!*" Only Willard had known that the singing ministry was not completely fulfilling for me. Oh, and of course God also knew.

"The ministry was fulfilling to you because of your family," Dan said, smiling. "But God wants you to have your own identity now and fulfillment in your own ministry."

A ministry? What on earth?

"The Lord is showing me that you have had a very bad hurt in your life. You've come through a dark time." Then he looked directly at me and asked, "Have you ever thought of writing a book?"

When that session closed, I couldn't dodge God's direction any longer. I had to trust that He was leading me into new directions, including something that seemed ridiculous to me: writing!

Not long after this, Youth With a Mission decided to have their first writing school in Tyler, Texas. One of the people who was putting it together approached me, "I hear you are thinking of writing, and I would like to encourage you to come to Texas and take the course." Even after all the Lord had showed me, I replied, "No, I don't think I will be writing." It all seemed so unreal to me. But after talking with me and hearing my story of how God had so clearly talked to me, she said to me, "LeeAnn, what does God have to do for you, throw tablets out of the sky at you?" She convinced me I should submit what I had written and see if I would be accepted at the school. Isn't it interesting how quickly we can doubt that God is speaking to us? I went to the school and there met David Hazard, who became my editor and encourager. Step by step, God made this book possible. I learned once again that our wonderful Lord is so trustworthy.

Now more then ten years later, God again has opened His wonderful heart and made it possible for me to rewrite this book. What a gift from Him to get a chance to add some new things!

The main point I want to make from this story is this: When unsettling times come, you can trust God to lead you. In fact, after suffering a devastating loss, your life can only become rich and rewarding again when you cast your cares upon God and trust Him to direct you. This means letting go of your fear, which really comes from a desire to control your life yourself.

Tell God you want to trust Him, you want Him to take charge of your life. Ask Him to take charge of your husband if you are emotionally or physically apart. If you're divorced or your husband has passed on, ask God to take charge of your loneliness. Give Him all that is in your life and ask Him to make it over anew. If you sense that inside you are really unwilling for this, ask Him to help you become willing.

But above all, don't sit and wait for the feeling of willingness to come over you, as if God has to let you know He's there by tickling your rib cage. Ask Him to guide you gently in the first steps you are to take in building your new life in Him. Finding God's plan for your life may not be easy when your head is clouded with loss. I know it wasn't easy for me at first. I so longed to have a deeper relationship with someone, to love and be loved. This thought seemed to occupy most of my waking moments.

In prayer one day, however, I realized God was speaking in the stillness of my heart. I heard the words, "Not until you are satisfied and fulfilled and content with being loved by Me alone!" I felt a stab of pain—and then a rush of joy. Yes, I would choose to trust Him to love me, no matter what came.

Before you try to run out and plan a new life for yourself, I caution you. Stop planning! Stop wishing! Allow Him to give you the most thrilling plan for your life, one you cannot even imagine. Be patient and wait, for He wants the very best for you. Look to Him every morning for what He wants to do in your life that day. You'll find He leads you one day and one step at a time. I've learned that when I live "simply" like this, He will give me the perfect peace He promises to all those who would follow Him (John 14). And one morning, He will awake you to surprises beyond your wildest dreams.

Let me tell you what He did for me.

Chapter Nine

God's Plan for You

From the outset, my purpose in this book has been to offer biblical principles that will help you fulfill an important part of God's will for you: to love your husband. Now I want to tell you how God continued to work out His plans for my life, even through dark and dismal times. This is my story, in brief, of what God has done for me since Willard's death. I describe this part of my life both to encourage you and because it illustrates a vital, scriptural principle every woman needs to know about God's will regarding her marriage and her husband.

Willard had been gone a little more than two years. It was summer, time for the harvest. I'd always loved harvest, but now it had lost its joy for me. It only made me lonely for my husband.

In many ways, life was sort of limping along. I'd had the brief discipleship training through YWAM, and I was scheduled to go on a short-term missionary venture in Asia in the fall. Mark and Laurie had been with YWAM for some months. In fact, Mark had had his own remarkable experiences with healing after the death of his dad.

While on the mission field, Mark had met another young man named Matt Rawlins who was teaching for YWAM. Matt was dealing with the fact that his mother was dying of cancer. Even the crackling phone connection that carried Mark's overseas call to me could not conceal the peace and joy Mark had found after this young man had discussed the Scriptures and prayed with him.

How I wished I felt that joy! The mission plans I'd made, good as they were, only filled up my waking hours. On one hand, I wanted to go to Asia. On the other hand, it was busyness, meant in part to help me avoid the empty hours that stretched before me, especially the nights—they were so long!

Occasionally, I would pull out a list I'd made some time after Willard's death and reread it. It was a list of all the qualities I wanted in a man if I ever remarried. Each time I reread the list, I suspected it would never happen. My qualifications seemed too specific, too lofty and demanding. The list went like this:

- He must be a man of God and not a new Christian. A spiritual leader.
- He must love my boys and have their approval.
- I'd like him to be handsome, fun-loving, and have a good sense of humor.
- I'd like him to be involved in missions. (This one troubled me a little, because Willard had left me well-off financially,

and I didn't want to use this money to support someone. A financially independent man, then—with a heart for missions? Maybe I was stretching it a little.)

- I'd like him to love traveling.
- It would probably be best if he had lost his mate, too. We would probably understand each other better if we both knew about this kind of loss and hurt.

Each time I reviewed the list, I had a sinking feeling. Surely there was no one anywhere who could fill this bill. I didn't want to make a mistake if I ever remarried, but maybe I'd given God too tall an order. Much of the time, I didn't think about my life or about remarrying at all. The hurt was too fresh. Maybe I'd remarry in three or four years—maybe longer. Most of my emotional energy went into making it from sunup to sundown.

Later in that "summer of the lonely harvest," some friends asked if I would be available to help with a YWAM training school at one of the mission's many bases, this one just forty miles from my home in Oregon. Knowing how I love to cook, they asked if I would help prepare meals. At first I hesitated. Then, knowing my son and our loyal employees could take care of the business, I decided it would do me good to get away again. That weekend, I made the drive.

Could This Be the One?

The man teaching on Monday morning was Duane Rawlins. Between rounds in the kitchen, I sat in on his classes. I quickly made some connections: Duane's son, Matt, was the young man who had lost his mom to cancer and had comforted my son, Mark, in his loss. It was nice to meet the father of such a godly young man. And I made some other unexpected connections, too.

Duane Rawlins was a real man of God, a spiritual leader who knew the Scriptures and was an excellent teacher. I learned that he owned several successful businesses, which allowed him the freedom to travel widely, teaching mostly for YWAM. He was also good-looking and athletic. When I heard him speak about the death of his wife, Betty, and how much it had affected him, I knew he was a sensitive man who felt pain deeply.

I was getting nervous.

That noon, our mutual friends introduced us. You're right to think they had something in mind! God took it from there.

Duane and I spent a lot of time together over the next few months. It didn't take us long to realize that it was God's desire for us to spend the rest of our lives together. Duane was everything on my list and more. When I told him that, he sheepishly pulled out his own list, one he'd written after Betty's death. That gave us both a good chuckle!

To make a long story short, we were married that Thanksgiving. The wedding was on a beach in Hawaii so that our children involved in missions in Asia and the others on the West Coast could all come. The marriage gave me three more exceptional children, Mark, Mindy, and Matt, plus their spouses, and it gave Duane and me a total of five grandchildren. My cup, which seemed so empty only months before, was full to overflowing.

Growing a Second Marriage

Duane and I have learned some basic lessons about love in a second marriage. Perhaps these lessons, which I'll explain briefly, will help others who are also entering into or are living in a second marriage.

First, a second marriage can become a time of starting over in your spiritual growth. Whether your first marriage ended by death or divorce, you are probably "a little older and a little wiser" regarding the important things in life. It seems that it takes loss and some hurt to teach us, doesn't it?

One of life's important things that I had always put aside during my years with Willard was to stay consistently in God's Word. As a Christian, I knew this was important. Even when we were involved in the music ministry, though, I always thought of consistent Bible reading and study as an obligation. Secretly, I sometimes felt it was a little like drudgery, though I'd never let anyone know that. In any case, I did not always consider it a joy. So I did what most of us do when we want to avoid something that's "good for us." I allowed life's busy details to crowd out time I could have spent with the Lord in His Word.

During my time in the Youth With a Mission Crossroads program, The Lord dealt with me and showed me the importance of daily meeting with Him on a consistent basis. I made a choice that year to do just that. Then I married Duane who had been practicing this for a number of years, making it easier for me to keep my commitment.

Now, together, Duane and I are committed to staying in God's Word daily. And I know my newfound consistency has come mostly from Duane's devotion to Bible study. We have entered into a kind of pact to study His Word, helping each other reach for new spiritual goals. I am convinced that our consistency in the Word has helped us often in the struggles of a second marriage. God is faithful and His Word is full of help for all our struggles.

A second lesson I learned is that it's possible to find as deep an intimacy in your second marriage as it was in your first.

For me, this came as I learned to be more free with my feelings when I talked to Duane—even my residual feelings of pain or joy when I'm reminded of Willard. Likewise, Duane says he has found freedom to share his lingering sorrow at thoughts of Betty's painful death, as well as wonderful memories that are so much a part of him.

In some second marriages we've observed, spouses don't allow each other to talk about previous husbands or wives, especially if there is anything good to say. Sometimes even stepchildren are not allowed to talk about the absent parent. We believe this is destructive. It's unrealistic to expect that someone your spouse once loved deeply should simply vanish from his or her emotional landscape, never to be mentioned again. Talking about your previous spouse, both the good and the bad, can only promote intimacy and bring comfort and assurance. It may be one of the healthiest things you can do for each other, and for your children.

A third lesson God has shown me is that I can still be flexible enough to be readjusted. I'd like to tell you that in the years Duane and I have been married, I've never had to make any adjustments to him. But I expect you wouldn't believe that anymore than I do.

Willard, as I've said before, was not very expressive with words. For twenty-four years, I was used to living with a man who would express his appreciation with a nod or a pat, and maybe a kiss. So I assumed that, unless Willard said he didn't like something I was doing (and it took quite a bit to get a rise out of him), I was okay. When I married Duane, a gifted communicator, I was in for a big adjustment.

I took pride in my cooking. Of course it took a major flop before Willard would scratch his chin and look at me questioningly. But those were few and far between—only a dry, tough pot roast here, a too-salty soup there. One day, however, not long after Duane and I married, I served up one of my breakfast favorites—my never-miss waffles. Duane almost always complimented my meals, so I was expecting some favorable comment as I sat down and picked up my fork.

Duane took a bite, then said casually, "These waffles are a bit soggy."

I was crushed. They were soggy, just a little, but Willard would never have said a word! It took a few minutes of silent reflection before I composed myself to see what was happening. I'd already promised myself I wouldn't compare Duane to Willard, but God wanted to teach me something more. I saw how set in my ways I'd become, how I expected things to be just the same.

I determined that morning that I would be flexible. Things would never be "like they were when I was married to Willard." I would allow God to bring into my life, along with a new husband, new opportunities for me to grow in even the smallest ways. I determined to make life with my second husband an adventure in growth, and that is what is has been.

God's Good Plans

I will relate a few more events in my life only to illustrate a larger truth that you, too, can live by. It doesn't matter whether your husband has passed away, has physically or emotionally abandoned you, or whether you are simply struggling with some rough spots in your relationship. I want you to hang onto a true word of encouragement; remembering it every morning and throughout the day as you pray for your husband and your relationship. It is this:

God will fulfill your dream of a wonderful marriage— and fulfill it beyond your wildest imagination—if only you will trust Him.

I can say this, not just because things worked out for me after my heartbreak, but also on the authority of Scripture. Listen to this wonderful promise from God our Father: "'For I know the plans I have for you,' declares the Lord, 'plans to prosper you and not to harm you, plans to give you hope and a future'" (Jer. 29:11 NIV).

It could be that you have never prayed and given your husband and your marriage relationship into God's hands. Or perhaps you made that commitment on your wedding day, and since then you've been fretting and trying to manage things your own way. I invite you now to bow your head and pray. Tell God you believe His promise for your marriage. Make Him the Lord of your marriage.

Give Him every little pocket of hurt or disappointment regarding your husband, and ask Him to fill it up with His forgiveness. Ask Him to make your marriage over—make it new!

You will never be sorry when you make this prayerful commitment before God. He always keeps His promises. You will also be amazed at the changes He brings in your own heart and the new kind of love you find there. And, as I've said before, you can't lose by loving. Try it and see.

Chapter Ten

Loving Your Husband in Life's Changing Seasons

A mother sent her older son out to pick berries in a wild patch of woods. The boy took nothing in which to carry the berries. You can imagine the condition when he got back home and emptied them on the table—out of his pockets!

His mother said, "Where is your common sense? The next time I send you to get something for me, have the presence of mind to carry it home in a box."

Two days later, she sent him off to find his four-year-old brother who was playing at the home of a friend.

I'll bet you've already guessed the punch line. The older brother returned home with his little brother—kicking and screaming inside a big cardboard box.

Sometimes we all need to be reminded that the methods that worked yesterday may not help us out today or tomorrow. Life changes. Circumstances change. People change.

One of the greatest mistakes we can make as wives is to be inflexible and resist change. You will be doing yourself a big favor if you'll remember that even your relationship with your husband is ever changing. Perhaps you're thinking, Oh, no! My love for him will *never* change. I'll always love him just the way I do today! Or perhaps that news makes you happy. Maybe you've been going through a trying period in your marriage, and you can't see even a hint of light in the darkness.

Let me assure you, every marriage goes through its changes and seasons. You may have a constantly good relationship and never go through a rough spell. But your emotional needs and your ability to give to one another will shift. Or, as I suggested, you may be thinking that things will never get better between you.

In either case, I want to help you see some of the changes that may yet lie ahead for you. I also want to help you understand how to love your husband best during these different seasons of life. We don't have to be like the boy in the story; we can be prepared to change the way we love to meet our changing needs and circumstances.

The Newlywed Season

The first season you'll encounter is the period when you and your husband are newlyweds. By this I don't mean the very beginning of your married life; I mean the time when you wake up in bed one morning, roll over, look at the guy next to you (the one snoring loudly enough to make the neighbor's dog bark) and think with an edge of panic, I'm married to this man!

Once the rose-pink blush of early bliss fades into the mundane grays and browns of everyday life, you begin to realize that you really and truly are married. That is, you are wed for life—not to a dreamy Prince Charming who meets all your emotional, physical, and financial needs, but to a guy who sometimes wants to fish all by himself or who asks you to move away from the TV so he won't miss the next kickoff. This is as rude an awakening for many women as it was for me.

You can respond to this "inner dawning" in several ways that will help your love to remain strong. Of course, these responses can apply in every season of marriage, but the earlier you learn them, the better off you'll be.

The best response you can work on is to look for the good in your husband and your circumstances. The apostle Paul put it this way: "...whatever is admirable—if anything is excellent or praiseworthy—think about such things" (Phil. 4:8 NIV). Because we're human, and because we go into marriage with the kind of high expectations I talked about earlier, we often focus on the negative. This is a fleshly, non-Christian response that we can learn to turn around.

Let's say you always wanted to marry a man who could support you and your children. Perhaps the guy you married was low-man on the ladder of a small company, but you could see that he had a lot of potential. You hoped that before long you could quit your job to stay at home and raise the children or pursue other personal interests.

After five years of marriage, however, you wake up to the fact that other men in your husband's company are climbing the ladder, but he seems satisfied with his lower position. So one day you ask him why he isn't getting the raises and promotions.

"I like what I do," he says with a shrug. "I'm not one of these guys who wants to claw his way to the top. You gotta' do a lot of things you don't believe in if you want a key to the executive suite. That's not for me. Most of those guys have high blood pressure."

You may find yourself facing this or a similar situation. Whatever you've just awakened to, you now know you are married to a man who will probably never fully meet some inner hope or dream you have.

Here are two bits of advice. First, sit down with pen and paper and list all the good things about your husband. Focus on all that is praiseworthy, or the things you find negative will grow like weeds and choke out your love.

Second, burn all your bridges to the past. Stop comparing your husband to the other men you might have married. And stop measuring him against all the dreams you've held since you were a little girl. Face yourself in the mirror and say, "He will never be all that I hoped, and that's okay. I will love him as he is, because that is what I promised in my wedding vows." Even if he criticizes your cooking!

Waking up to disappointment is waking up to who *you* are. It's realizing the limits of your love. It's finding out how small and petty human love is. In the end, we all demand to have what we want. And that's a good point to come to, for when we see how self-centered we are, we can ask God to fill our unloving and inflexible hearts with His love. Only when you have reached this point, have you found a solid platform on which to build your marriage.

God's love is the foundation that will make any marriage steadfast and strong—if only we will ask Him for that love. And when we ask, He gives His love freely and in abundant measure (Luke 6:38).

The Child Rearing Season

Another season of marriage is the season of child rearing. Adding children to a marriage throws some big challenges at you.

One of the first is the tendency a woman has to put her children before her husband. It's easy to slip into this. Children are so needy when they're small, and always so demanding. One day it seems you and your husband are enjoying quiet walks together along forested paths, or candlelit dinners for two. And then it hits. A child enters the picture and wrings every last ounce of love, patience, and energy out of you.

If you're in the early stages of child rearing, I must encourage you. It gets easier. You may not believe it now, but there will soon come a time when you are not on call twenty-four hours a day.

Even when it seems you are so busy with your little ones, don't neglect their needs and interests. As I look back at my days of raising my little boys I never think, "Sure wish I would not have spent so much time listening to their sweet questions." I know if you are in the middle of changing those never-ending diapers, it seems like the time will never come when there are not soggy wet diapers on your little ones. But I am here to tell you, before you turn around these little guys will be in college, then married, and soon will be changing the soggy diapers on their little ones. Value those priceless times together.

But again I must warn you to not forget your husband. Allow him to help you with them, even if you don't like the way he puts their diapers on. Be careful not to expect help from him when he has worked hard all day. But be sure to thank him and let him know how much it blesses you when he does help even in the smallest ways. Just a hint to you husbands—you will never know how even the smallest offer of help will bless your wife more than you could possibly know. It puts good things upstream in her heart.

No matter how old your children are, I also want to encourage you to do this: Save something of yourself to give to your husband. There is no law saying that in order to be a good Christian mother, you must give yourself so totally to your children that you feel like a wrung-out dishrag at the end of the day.

(There will be enough days when you feel like that anyway!) Most husbands need just a little attention from someone who will stop long enough to give them a squeeze and a wink and say, "I love you, and I'm glad you're home."

Here are some simple ways you can love your husband during those seemingly endless years of child rearing:

- A man needs to know he is a good provider. Give him the gift of a few words of gratitude.
- A man needs to know his thoughts and values are important. Give him the gift of a few minutes of undivided attention. Ask his opinion, and tell him why it's helpful to you.
- A man needs to know you and his children respect him. Give him the gift of a few words of praise. When your children are present, mention one of his traits that you admire.
- A man needs to know he can be himself, even when he comes up short. Give him the gift of confidence and confidentiality. It takes only a moment to say, "I forgive you, and I love you no matter what."
- A man needs a woman who is strong, who is growing toward godly maturity. Give him the gift of spending time with God each day so you are becoming more like Christ. Find your fulfillment not in a career or children or even in your husband; *find it by growing in the Lord.*

Perhaps the most important thing to learn during the busy, demanding season of child rearing is this: Sow small acts and words of love, patiently and constantly, the way a farmer plants seeds, and you will reap a continual harvest of love from your man.

I remember some precious times when the boys were small, and I'd bundle them up so we could all go with Willard in the truck while he ran some errand. It was a little thing, but it showed him I wanted to be with him even when it was sometimes inconvenient. And such little things add up.

Another part of the child rearing season is being able to let go of your children when they grow up. This is one reason it is so important to have a close relationship with their father. The children are with us for a season, but time goes on with a husband and wife. This will make letting go of your children so much easier.

For me it was hard to let go of my first son, Mark, when he decided to go to college and then get married. But it made it easier because I had his dad as my best friend. Then when it was time for our second and third sons to get married, it was a different story. Willard had died the year before, and releasing Lonnie was so hard. Then when the time came to release our youngest son, Rob, it was also hard, but by then I was remarried and had my present husband, Duane, to help make this process easier. But as I have said before, God gives you the grace to do what you have to do when you have to do it, if you will receive that grace. I wish I had taken advantage of that grace more at the time. I learned the hard way that if we will release our children, they will return to us in an even more fulfilling way.

One morning I sat thinking, What now? It was only a few weeks ago that Mark and Laurie had come to Willard and me and told us they were praying about going with Youth With a Mission for a few months. What did we think about that, they asked us? As I sat thinking back, I remembered we really hadn't had much time to discuss it at all. I do remember reasoning that it might be just the thing we were wishing for the kids. They could remove themselves from the farm for a short term, though they really did want to be farmers. We were so looking forward to the day when we would be able to turn things over to the boys and do some short-term mission work ourselves. It did seem so logical for them to step into the farm business, but we had learned from some of our friends'experiences that we really must release our children to do what they feel God is calling them to do, and not what we desired for them to do or what "seemed best." So this might be just the thing for them.

We were beginning to get excited...then it happened—Willard was gone. As I sat there thinking, I reasoned, "God, no matter how good that seemed to us, all has changed now—everything is different. I need them here so badly!" Willard had left me with three businesses. But as the months wore on, I realized Mark and Laurie really did need to remove themselves from all that had been put on them so suddenly, now probably more than ever. So with much hesitation and trying hard to trust God fully, I gave them my blessing to go. Needless to say they were thrilled, and six months after Willard died they were off to New Zealand for three months in Discipleship Training School.

It was so hard to see them go. It did help to have my second son, Lonnie, who was in his second year of premed school move back home with me for that term. Another blessing from the Lord. I will always be grateful to him for being willing to leave his independence and return home again. We had good managers in each of our businesses—another blessing from God—but I still needed Mark's help so often. Yet their letters were full of enthusiasm which pleased me that they could be in New Zealand. Then the phone call came. After the three months training in YWAM, they wanted to go on an outreach, wherever the Lord lead them. They called from New Zealand and said they felt God calling them to the Philippines. I was sure the connection was bad. The Philippines?! I had just heard that there was unrest there. "God, are you there? I let them go to New Zealand because that seemed safe, but God, not the Philippines!" I was silent then. I said, "Mark, how can God be calling you to the Philippines? He is not telling me that for you." After some discussion I ended with, "Honey, I just can't send the money to support you to go there." I reluctantly told him I would pray about it. I am sure he was disappointed, and I felt a heavy heart as I hung up the phone. I cried for several days asking, "God, why? Why? Hadn't I allowed Mark and Laurie to go? Wasn't that enough?" It was awful. "Lord, help me find peace."

That weekend I attended a baby dedication for my niece's baby. The pastor said, "You know when our babies are small we say, 'Lord, wherever You want them to go, they are Yours. Use them. Timbuktu or wherever.' But when they grow up and God asks them to go to Timbuktu or wherever we say, 'NO!'" It hit me. I slumped down in my seat. I didn't have a choice. Willard and I had dedicated Mark to the Lord and had made that choice some 20 years ago. A peace flooded over me. I could hardly wait to get home and phone Mark to tell him what God had done and that the large sum of money saved for outreach would be in the mail the next morning. I made the call, and as I shared this with Mark, there was silence on the line. I asked him, "What is wrong?" It took him a minute to recover. Then he shared with me how happy it made him, and though he knew he did not need my consent he did want my blessing. The story did not end there. He shared with me that God had already supplied the funds he needed. And that just blessed me. God does not need our money. He owns the cattle on a thousand hills (Ps. 50:10). He only wants our willing hearts.

This experience was such an incredible thing for me, and since then God has put a wonderful peace in my heart about any of our children going out. Again, He never fails us.

The Mid-life Season

A third season in your love for your husband comes in mid-life. In fact, for your husband, this may be the time when he most needs your love.

Today, we hear a lot about men who reach mid-life—that is, their forties and fifties—only to hit an emotional crisis. Popularly, it's called "a mid-life crisis," and it's characterized by a man's loss of confidence, mourning of missed opportunities, restlessness, or a sudden change of behavior. But even if mid-life is not a time of major upheaval for your husband, it will most likely be a time when he reassesses his life. He may seem to be pulling away from you. It will almost certainly be a time when he needs your love in a new and different way.

If your husband has reached mid-life and his boat seems to be rocking a little, your love can be a steadying influence. Naturally, by mid-life you will have gotten used to your husband's habits and mannerisms. If you sense a sudden change, especially restlessness, your first response may be panic. You may think, "He's unsatisfied with me."

At this point, you may try desperately to assure yourself of his love by forcing yourself into his arms and his most private thoughts. But your efforts will only be an attempt to hear words you want to hear, to be assured that nothing has changed. You may feel as if *your* emotional boat is rocking, too, and that you are trying to steady things for yourself and not for him at all.

First, the best way to love your husband in this season of mid-life reassessment is to remember that he needs you to be stable. I'm not suggesting this is easy, because any changes he makes also affect you. But if you focus only on yourself and not on his needs, you'll never have the chance to help him through this rough period.

Second, you can remind your husband of all he has accomplished in his life so far. It's common for men in mid-life—even men who once seemed contented—to suddenly be seized with an overwhelming remorse. They may think of all the career opportunities they could have taken, or all of the things they could have done with their children. They may even relive long-past mistakes they "should never have made."

It's important that you don't make his lost dreams or missed opportunities seem trivial. Don't say, "Oh, it doesn't matter that you're not chairman of the board." To him, at that moment, it matters. You must gently, consistently remind him of all he has accomplished. This will be a lot easier if you've spent time focusing on his good points. The fact that you value his life and accomplishments will help him regain perspective.

You may also feel threatened and sense that a major change is coming. Your husband suddenly starts talking about moving to a distant city, joining the Foreign Legion, or quitting his high-paying job to open a surf shop in the Bahamas. He may even suggest, in his desperation to find himself, that you separate.

Even if he doesn't suggest uprooting your comfortable life to do something drastic or crazy, let him know you're with him all the way. Tell him, in the words of Ruth:

> But Ruth replied, "Don't urge me to leave you or to turn back from you. Where you go I will go, and where you stay I will stay. Your people will be my people and your God my God. Where you die I will die, and there I will be buried. May the Lord deal with me, be it ever so severely, if anything but death separates you and me."
>
> Ruth 1:16-17 NIV

So many of us wrote those words into our wedding ceremonies. We stood and gazed into the eyes of our young bridegroom and vowed to him with all our heart. Now, in mid-life, we need to take stock of promises made in our youth. And we need to renew our courage to live by them.

A friend once described a mid-life crisis he and his wife went through and how they handled it. As the years went by in their marriage, he became more and more involved in his work, often being away from home on business for several days at a time. She became more and more wrapped up in their children. Gradually a deadening of feelings occurred in both of them. The red tape of duty took over their relationship, and the intimacy disappeared.

Then one day, on a business trip plane ride, the husband met a young woman whose husband had recently left her for another woman. Because of his love for people and his skills in counseling, our friend talked with her. The next day, he called to see how she was doing and spent an hour on the phone with her. Perhaps because of the safety of being on the phone or his own deep need for affection, he began to discuss his own feelings, and consequently he experienced a warmth he had been missing for several years.

Suddenly, he was overwhelmed and frightened by the thoughts he found going through his head about this woman. He told me later that he was so grateful he had been in a telephone booth at that time and not in the woman's house.

Being a Christian who was still deeply committed to his wife, in spite of the coldness in their relationship, he chose to go home and tell her about the whole experience. And she proved to be a wise and loving mate, listening empathetically rather than critically, admitting her own vulnerability. As a result, what could have been a disaster, instead became a means of drawing them together and renewing their determination to keep their marriage fresh and exciting.

The Senior Season

The other season most of us will face with our husbands is the senior years.

I must say these are wonderful years for me. Other than the normal aging process, it really is a great time. Like any season in your marriage, most of your happiness is what you make of what life hands you. Duane and I are enjoying being able to do things together whenever we feel like it, and not having to worry about the daily business. We have retired, but we like to think we have really "re-fired." I realize retiring can be a very hard thing for your husband, especially. Stand by him and help him understand that just because he does not go to work every day does not mean he has no worth.

Both of you can get into the Word more. Share it with others. There are so many opportunities to volunteer. You will be most fulfilled when you are reaching out to others. Do things together. Enjoy these senior years by loving each other and those around you.

I know that more than likely one of us will end up taking care of whoever is healthier. But isn't that what we promised, through sickness and in health? I learned a long time ago that God will give us the grace to do whatever we need to do if we are just willing to receive it. As for now, we are enjoying good health and a good life. God has opened up so many opportunities for us. These senior years are great years for us right now. And we are confident that should things change, His grace will be sufficient.

One of the most blessed rewards of senior years is the grandchildren with whom God graces your life. I truly did love being mom, but this grandma stuff is just wonderful! At the time of this writing, we have fourteen grandchildren, and number fifteen will join us this summer. There are so many wonderful blessings that we get to enjoy as grandparents. Grandchildren are the joy of our senior years. Just to see their eyes light up when they come to see us is priceless. Enjoy your children and grandchildren. You must remember you will probably leave your greatest legacy through them. Cherish and love them. Do things together with them. Ask yourself this question, "When was the last time I spent a solid hour playing with my grandchildren or spent time reading to them?" Ask your grandchildren what kinds of things they would like to do with you. There is so much grandparents can give to these very special little people. These memories are put in an emotional bank account that they can draw from for the rest of their lives. It means so much to them. One of the fun things I have done for our grandchildren was to make a trunk full of dress-up clothes. They love to dress up and put on little plays for us. Sometimes they go to the front door all dressed up and come in for tea with me. Help them be creative. With television and all the "things" kids have these days, they need to be encouraged to be creative.

If you do not have grandchildren or yours do not live close to you, adopt some. These little ones need you and you need them. The greatest need for anyone, especially a child, is to feel that he or she is loved and special. We all know that the best way to give anyone a nurtured feeling is to give him or her your undivided time and attention. There is the deepest emotional nurturing done during one-on-one times of bonding together. The greatest benefit for us grandparents is that during these times, we do not have to lecture or teach. We just need to listen and understand. Let your grandchild help plan these special times together. The anticipation of the "special time" is as great as the realization of that actual time spent together. In today's world so many grandparents are having a very important role in their grandchildren's lives because of the busy lives of their parents. Don't miss this wonderful input in their lives.

This senior season can be a gentle and yet stimulating time as your love moves into another phase. At this time, you will be called upon to love your husband in the face of both new challenges and promises.

One challenge a man may face is the feeling that he has outlived his usefulness. A man's identity is so bound up with what he does and accomplishes (as opposed to what kind of person he is) that most feel they are being forced to retire—that they're being put out to pasture.

These men respond by becoming restless and irritable. They don't want to sit still and do nothing. They hate the idea of retiring to Florida to play shuffleboard and golf every day. Some wives simply make themselves scarce, or they warn the grandchildren to stay away because, "Grandpa is in one of his cranky moods."

On the other hand, it may be that your husband eagerly volunteers to take an early retirement. His calendar is filled with plans for fishing ventures and cross-country trips. Yet many of these men quickly find the free life of retirement boring and empty. This is the time when a wife can gently walk alongside her husband, pointing out the other kinds of productive things he can do. I am talking about things that will continue to build Christlikeness in him.

Primarily, you can encourage your husband to let his gifts of wisdom shine. Help him tally up all his years of experience in areas like family leadership, business, even sports and leisure activities. Encourage him to put his practical knowledge to work, serving others who may need guidance in these areas. Let him know he still has many jobs left to accomplish. Now his life's work need not be work, but joy and service to others.

Some dear friends retired early from their employment, though both were still active and full of life. They took an extended vacation to Hawaii, and while on the Big Island, they went to visit someone who was attending YWAM's Pacific and Asia Christian University. Their friend was gone that day, but since they were there, the couple decided to tour the college anyway.

What they saw excited them so much that they soon found themselves enrolled in a Crossroads discipleship class at the university. That training in turn motivated them to get involved with the university's program for helping other middle-aged and older people who were at crossroads in their lives. For about a year they served happily together in this new ministry. By thus encouraging her husband, the wife gave him a fresh sense of purpose in his later years.

The senior years can also be a time of special openness to one another. Health problems and a limited income need not be causes for fear and stress. They, too, can be tools to draw you together in prayer, dialogue, and spiritual growth.

Don't waste these great years together. Life can be so full and rich if we just allow it to be. Always keep in mind that circumstances do not determine our happiness. Our life is often as wonderful or as awful as we make it to be.

Choose to Love

The one principle that applies in all seasons of life is this: You can live according to God's directives and choose to love. Your love for your husband does not have to be a wishy-washy, change-with-the-weather kind of thing. That kind of love turns to mush when things get tough.

Whether you are going through a peaceful or a challenging season with your husband right now, God has a high calling for you. Your love, patience, and service will help your husband through hard times. Your enthusiasm and support will also help him, in God's good timing, to become more the man God wants him to be.

Whatever your situation, God can help you be your husband's best friend, a woman of strength, growing in maturity. Isn't that what you really want?

So rejoice in the season you are in. Let the Lord give you the grace you need to walk through it. Let Him walk with you through whatever you are going through and in whatever season you are in. I have discovered that there are some good seasons and some not-so-good seasons we all go through. It is not the season, but how we go through that season that counts.

Notes

Chapter 1

1. *Guinness Book of World Records* (New York: Bantam Books, 1998), 27.
2. www.divorcereform.org/results.html, April 1999.

Chapter 4

1. Larry Crab, *Connecting* (Nashville, Tenn.: Thomas Nelson Publishers, 1997), 32.
2. From *Focus on the Family* radio broadcast, March 1999.

Chapter 5

1. Crab, 152.
2. Alan Loy McGinnis, *The Friendship Factor* (Minneapolis, Minn.: Augsburg Publishing House, 1979), 11.
3. Erich Segal, *Love Story* (New York: Harper and Row Publishers, Inc., 1970), 141.

Chapter 6

1. www.divorcereform.org/results.html, April 1999.

Chapter 7

1. Ann Kaiser, ed., "Whether You're a Widow or Not...Please Read This Page," *Farm Wife News 14, no.4* (April 1984): 24. Reprinted by permission.